CHOOSE
Kindness

3-MINUTE DEVOTIONS
FOR TEEN GIRLS

Our mission is to inspire the world with the life-changing message of the Bible.

Member of the
Evangelical Christian
Publishers Association

CHOOSE
Kindness

3-MINUTE DEVOTIONS FOR TEEN GIRLS

KRISTIN WEBER

BARBOUR BOOKS
An Imprint of Barbour Publishing, Inc.

Dear Reader,

I'm so glad you picked up this book! It means that you care about something the world currently needs more of: kindness. A kind person stands out in a culture overrun with bullying, meanness, and anger.

In this book, you'll find more than 180 devotions to encourage you as you choose daily to live a life of kindness. You may notice the prayers in each devotion don't have an "amen" at the end. Think of them as a conversation starter between you and God. When the devotion ends, continue talking to God throughout the day!

You are loved, sweet sister, and my prayer is that through the pages of this book you'll grow closer to our Lord Jesus, whose kindness toward us in what He did on the cross motivates us to extend kindness to others.

May God bless you as you seek to be a light in the darkness!

Kristin Weber

To Be Kind

*She opens her mouth with wisdom, and the
teaching of kindness is on her tongue.*
PROVERBS 31:26 ESV

What does it mean to be kind? And what does a life of kindness look like?

A kind person seeks the well-being of others through their words, attitude, and actions. A kind person learns to value peace and harmony over retaliation and anger. A kind person listens quickly, speaks gently, and loves fiercely. A kind person shows mercy and compassion to anyone in need.

You won't accidentally stumble into a life of kindness. It's a path that must be chosen and traveled carefully. A life of kindness takes determination, discipline, and grace. When you choose kindness, Jesus shines through your life, beckoning the world to a hope greater than anything found on this earth.

. . . .

*Dear Lord, I want to choose kindness.
Send Your Spirit to fill me with kindness so
that other people might come to know You.*

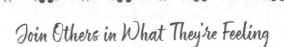

Join Others in What They're Feeling

Be happy with those who are happy,
and weep with those who weep.
ROMANS 12:15 NLT

Imagine you have incredibly exciting news—you got the lead in the school play, you're going on an awesome vacation, or you won concert tickets to see your favorite singer. When you tell your friend your news though, her response is simply, "That's cool," and then she changes the subject.

Now imagine you're having a tough day. You tell your friend that you're sad and anxious, and her response is simply, "But you have so many good things in your life. Focus on those instead of being sad!"

Hopefully, your friends respond better than that, because one expression of kindness is joining others in what they're feeling. By celebrating with someone when something amazing happens, or quietly sitting next to them and listening when they're sad, we visibly show the love of Jesus.

Dear Lord, please give me the ability to notice
when others are going through something and
to join them in their celebration or sadness.

Spiritual Clothes

*Therefore, as God's chosen people, holy and
dearly loved, clothe yourselves with compassion,
kindness, humility, gentleness and patience.*
COLOSSIANS 3:12 NIV

How much time does it take you to pick out what to wear in the morning? (Or in the afternoon on school breaks and weekends!)

As you're thinking about how to dress your physical body each day, reflect on how to clothe yourself spiritually. How can you put on kindness, compassion, humility, gentleness, and patience today?

* *

*Dear God, it's so easy to only focus
on my outer appearance. Help me
remember to clothe myself spiritually.*

Speak of What Others Have Done for You

*"But when all goes well with you, remember
me and show me kindness; mention me to
Pharaoh and get me out of this prison."*
GENESIS 40:14 NIV

Have you read the story of Joseph in the Bible? After being sold into slavery by his brothers, he was falsely accused of a crime and got thrown into prison. While there, Joseph helped interpret the dreams of two prisoners, a cupbearer and baker, who both worked for Pharaoh. (Pharaoh was the Egyptian ruler.)

Pharaoh put the baker to death but restored the cupbearer to his position. Unfortunately, the cupbearer forgot to mention Joseph to Pharaoh, and Joseph stayed in prison for two more years.

It's important to remember what others have done for us and to speak of their gifts to others, especially if doing so helps them out. The stakes may not be as high as getting someone out of wrongful imprisonment, but the simple act of remembering shows incredible kindness.

. . . .

Dear Jesus, sometimes I forget what others have done for me. Help me to remember other people and to do what I can to help them out in both my words and actions.

Confess Your Sins to Each Other

Make this your common practice: Confess your sins to each other and pray for each other so that you can live together whole and healed.
JAMES 5:16 MSG

Have you ever done something wrong and thought, *Well, nobody saw what I did, so I can just keep it to myself and no one will ever know!*

God doesn't want us to shove our sin into a drawer and forget about it. Keeping sin in the dark brings guilt, shame, and sometimes even more sin.

Confessing your sins both to God and to others brings healing and spiritual freedom. In fact, sharing your struggles and victories can uniquely encourage other believers. By sharing your story, you could help bring wholeness and healing to others.

. . . .

Lord Jesus, confessing my sins is scary. What if people judge me or make fun of me? Give me the courage to confess my struggles to those who will understand, and help me conquer my sin.

Forgive as Christ Forgave You

Bear with each other and forgive one another
if any of you has a grievance against someone.
Forgive as the Lord forgave you.
COLOSSIANS 3:13 NIV

Conflicts happen, even among Christians. Sometimes it stings worse when a Christian friend hurts us because we often hold those following Jesus to a higher standard. We must choose to let things go, to forgive, and to be gentle toward fellow believers who hurt or offend us.

If you're struggling to forgive someone today, think about how God forgave you: freely, fully, and before you even knew you'd sinned. If a brother or sister in Christ hurts you, forgive quickly and trust that the Holy Spirit is working on their heart, just like He's working on yours.

· ·

Why is forgiveness so hard, God? Help me let go
of the anger and hurt I feel, especially toward
people who share my faith in You.

Bear Each Other's Burdens

Bear one another's burdens,
and so fulfill the law of Christ.
GALATIANS 6:2 ESV

Sometimes bearing a burden means taking care of someone's physical needs, such as babysitting, helping with household chores, or bringing meals. Other times, it means showing up during a difficult time, even when you don't know what to say or do.

People often steer clear of those going through trials because they're afraid of saying or doing the wrong thing. It's incredibly kind to brave the awkwardness that comes with difficult situations and say, "I don't know what to say, but I'm so sorry. I'm here, and I want to help."

We might not be able to fix someone's situation, but we can help keep it from crushing them by being present.

* *

Dear Lord, help me be there for people when they're hurting. Give me the wisdom to know what to say and do so I can shoulder the burdens of those around me.

No One Beneath You

Live in harmony with one another. Do not be
proud, but be willing to associate with people
of low position. Do not be conceited.
ROMANS 12:16 NIV

If you look around a high school cafeteria, you can quickly see where everyone fits in. Musicians sit with their friends from orchestra, athletes sit with other athletes, and the popular kids all clump together in their cliques.

But what about those who don't belong to a certain table? Think of the hurt and pain when you aren't considered "good enough" to sit with a particular group.

Everyone wants popularity, friends, and to sit at the "cool" table. These are completely normal desires. However, we must be quick to include people who don't have a place to sit. Jesus extended friendship to the lowest members of society. Each day brings the opportunity to follow His example and include those the world wants to leave out.

Father God, help me see those who need a
friend. Give me boldness to approach
them and invite them to my table.

Consider Your Source

*"This is my commandment: Love each
other in the same way I have loved you."*
JOHN 15:12 NLT

The best chefs purchase ingredients for their restaurants from high-quality sources. The source of the ingredients affects the outcome of the dish, so they're picky about their suppliers.

Jesus loved us by becoming our *source* of joy, kindness, hope, healing, love, forgiveness, salvation, self-control, and peace. What He offers is much, much higher quality than what the world offers.

. . . .

*I want to love others in the same way You love me,
Jesus. Fill me up so that I can become a source
of hope and love for those around me!*

Lay Down Your Life

*"Greater love has no one than this, that
someone lay down his life for his friends."*
JOHN 15:13 ESV

Jesus set the bar incredibly high when it came to loving others. He loved us so much that He willingly died on the cross so we could be cleansed of our sins.

Jesus also laid down His life while living, putting aside His own comfort to follow God and serve others. You may never be asked to die for your friends, but you can still lay down your life for them by following Jesus' example in living sacrificially.

Think about what you could surrender in order to love others better. You could lay down your time, forgoing video games and Netflix binges to volunteer somewhere. You could lay down your comfort to bring Christ to unreached people. Or maybe you can lay down your plans for the day in order to be present for a friend in need.

* * *

*Dear God, open my eyes to ways I can lay down my life
for my friends. Reveal to me the selfishness in my life,
and help me put my own desires aside to love others.*

Keep Your Eyes Forward

*Make it your goal to live a quiet life, minding
your own business and working with your
hands, just as we instructed you before.*

1 THESSALONIANS 4:11 NLT

There are many times when it's right and good to step
in and help someone in need. Sometimes though, the
kindest and wisest thing you can do is mind your own
business and keep living your life peacefully.

For example, if you hear a piece of gossip floating
around, don't become curious and try to find out more.
Before long, instead of "helping" the situation, you'll
actually start contributing to the problem.

Instead, step away from gossip. Unless you're in a
position to say something that stops it, don't feed the
flames of slander and meanness. Instead, walk away and
go do something productive and meaningful with your
time.

. . . .

*Dear God, I'm sorry for the times I've gotten involved
in things that were none of my business. Help me
walk away from gossip and spend my time wisely.*

Encourage Good Works

And let us consider how to stimulate
one another to love and good deeds.
HEBREWS 10:24 NASB

Recently, a friend at my church shared with me how she got up the courage to tell one of her neighbors about Jesus. Her boldness to speak truth, even though it was uncomfortable at first, inspired me to look for more ways to share Christ. Her actions stirred me to good works.

You never know the impact an act of kindness or obedience has on those around you. Your gentle words might make someone stop and think about how they've been treating others. Your willingness to forgive someone who's wronged you might help someone let go of a grudge they've been carrying. Never pass up an opportunity to do good, for a single act of kindness may push back the darkness for ages to come.

. . . .

Heavenly Father, make my words and actions
stir others to do good works in Your name.

Don't Give Up

*Let us not become weary in doing good, for at the
proper time we will reap a harvest if we do not give up.*
GALATIANS 6:9 NIV

While visiting Costa Rica this past summer, I learned
that it takes three to four years before a coffee plant
produces any usable beans. That's a lot of waiting and
preparation before getting anything in return!

Sometimes kindness doesn't feel like it's making a
difference. Perhaps the people you help aren't grateful,
take advantage of you, or see you as a pushover. The
reality is this: doing good gets tiring when you don't see
positive results.

Don't lose heart, dear sister. Your kindness now
might be preparing the soil for future fruit. Obedience
always reaps blessing, just not always on our timetable.
While you wait for your earthly harvest, remember that
Jesus sees your obedience and prepares your ultimate
reward in heaven.

• •

*Dear Jesus, it's so hard to keep doing the right thing
and never see anything good come out of it. I'm
going to try and continue doing good works, even
when they don't seem to be making a difference.*

Learn to Love Kindness

He has told you, O man, what is good; and what does the LORD require of you but to do justice, and to love kindness, and to walk humbly with your God?
MICAH 6:8 ESV

Take a moment and think about recent opportunities you've had to show kindness to others. Did you show kindness out of obligation, or because other people were watching and you wanted to look good? Or did you extend kindness because you love being kind?

Sometimes the first step to *loving* something is *doing* it, even if the feelings aren't quite there yet. Maybe you already love kindness, or maybe you don't see the point. By trusting the Lord and obeying His command for kindness, you'll eventually fall in love with the joy that comes with doing good. Kindness will take root in your life, and the resulting fruit will bless everyone in your circle.

- -

*Dear Jesus, please give me
a genuine love of kindness.*

Use Your Gift to Serve Others

God has given each of you a gift from
his great variety of spiritual gifts.
Use them well to serve one another.
1 PETER 4:10 NLT

When God adopted you, He equipped you with a gift (or several!) to build up other believers. Your personality, patience with children, joy, sense of humor, eye for detail, ability to teach, artistic skills, knack for organization, or whatever else you possess were given to you by God to serve and expand His kingdom.

Think about the gifts you have to share with your church. No gift is too small or less important. If you're using what God gave you to serve Him, you're blessing your brothers and sisters in the Lord and bringing joy to the heart of God.

I want to use my talents to serve You, Lord.
Reveal to me my gifts, and provide me with
opportunities to use them for Your kingdom.

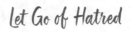

Let Go of Hatred

"You shall not hate your brother in your heart,
but you shall reason frankly with your neighbor,
lest you incur sin because of him."
LEVITICUS 19:17 ESV

When someone mistreats you, it's natural to be upset. Still, confronting people isn't fun. It would be much easier if the person who hurt you figured out what they did wrong and apologized on their own, right?

Most people want to avoid conflict. Instead of gently pointing out how someone hurt us, we often hold on to the pain and let it turn into anger or hate. When we hate, we become the ones sinning against God and hurt our own spiritual growth.

Rather than hold a grudge, lovingly try to reconcile with the person who hurt you. They may not be open to making up, but your conscience will be clear knowing you did your part to maintain peace.

. . . .

Father God, I know it's wrong to hate someone
in my heart. Give me the right words to say
when someone hurts me, and help me let go of any
anger if they aren't sorry for what they've done.

Picking Favorites

If a man enters your church wearing an expensive suit,
and a street person wearing rags comes in right after
him, and you say to the man in the suit, "Sit here, sir;
this is the best seat in the house!" and either ignore the
street person or say, "Better sit here in the back row,"
haven't you segregated God's children and proved
that you are judges who can't be trusted?
JAMES 2:2–4 MSG

Think about how excited you'd be if your favorite actor
or athlete came and sat next to you at church. You'd be
thrilled, and if you weren't too starstruck, you'd probably want to help them connect and make sure they felt
welcome. (And maybe snag a selfie with them.)

Would you greet a stranger who dressed or acted
oddly with that same excitement and enthusiasm?
Would you make sure they felt welcome and included?
Christian kindness means stepping outside your comfort zone and making sure everyone—both rich and
poor, cool and uncool, famous and unknown—feels welcome and loved.

Dear Jesus, I don't want to show favoritism.
I need to see and welcome everyone as if they
were the most important person I've met.

Kindness in All Things

*For I can do everything through
Christ, who gives me strength.*
PHILIPPIANS 4:13 NLT

The apostle Paul, who wrote this verse in his letter to the Philippian church, experienced all kinds of circumstances during his ministry. He went through times with plenty and times with nothing. He experienced persecution and acceptance. He knew that whatever he faced, he could do it with the strength of Christ.

Some days kindness will come easily. Other days, you won't feel like being kind at all. You'll be tired, sick, or in a bad mood and tempted to take out your frustrations on the people around you. In those moments, rely on the strength of Christ to help you love others.

*Dear God, give me Your strength on difficult
days. Even when I'm having a hard time,
make me obedient to Your call for kindness.*

Beautiful Mercy

*There will be no mercy for those who have
not shown mercy to others. But if you have been
merciful, God will be merciful when he judges you.*
JAMES 2:13 NLT

If you struggle to show compassion, take a moment and meditate on the incredible mercy you've been shown by God. Instead of leaving you to wallow in your sins, God extended compassion and mercy. He entered the messiness of the world by sending Jesus to live perfectly, die horrifically, and conquer death with the resurrection. Because of this, nothing you've done will be held against you if you put your trust in Christ. You're a completely forgiven child of God!

This is great mercy, and a person who's been *shown* great mercy *shows* great mercy to others.

* *

*Heavenly Father, help me show compassion
and mercy to all who need it.*

Excitement Abounds

*Never be lacking in zeal, but keep
your spiritual fervor, serving the Lord.*
ROMANS 12:11 NIV

When I was a kid, I'd get really excited when my parents let me help them cook. I loved learning how to prepare meals and bake goodies—something I continue enjoying to this day.

God has invited you to help Him in His work. You get a front-row seat to watching God change and transform lives. *You*, His beloved daughter, get to assist your heavenly Father in sharing the good news of what He's done!

. . . .

*You've called me to great work, God! My
heart wants to serve You with excitement
and enthusiasm in every area of my life.*

All Kinds of Weather

*Friends love through all kinds of weather,
and families stick together in all kinds of trouble.*
PROVERBS 17:17 MSG

My grandmother used to warn me to be careful of "fair-weather friends." These friends loved to hang out when times were good, but the instant trouble or hardship came along, they disappeared.

Loving a friend means standing by their side both when things are sunny and when the storms of life rage. It means celebrating the good and throwing them a lifeline when tumultuous waters threaten to carry them away.

. . . .

*Dear Jesus, it's so important to be a good friend—
the kind who loves through all types of weather.
Please give me the strength to stand by my
friends through the good and bad.*

Hating Evil

Let love be without hypocrisy. Abhor
what is evil; cling to what is good.
ROMANS 12:9 NASB

We're sometimes taught that it's wrong to hate, but it's actually *good* to hate things God hates. Murder, oppression, injustice, and sin all deserve our hatred and disgust. These things offend and grieve God. Therefore, they should offend and grieve us as well.

If we claim to love people but ignore suffering and injustice, our love looks hypocritical to the world. By hating what's evil, we express love to those who've been wronged. Righteous anger drives us to speak up and act on behalf of those victimized and marginalized. It drives us to shine our light in the darkest places.

• •

Lord God, teach me to recognize and hate evil.
Help me cling to what's good and look for ways
to destroy what's wicked in Your eyes.

What Are Your Motives?

Do nothing from selfish ambition or conceit,
but in humility count others more
significant than yourselves.
PHILIPPIANS 2:3 ESV

"Aim higher! Push harder! Accomplish more!" This is a common message in today's world. We're told to get to the top, no matter the cost.

God's given you unique talents and goals. It's always a good idea, however, to do a "heart check" and ask yourself *why* you want to achieve something. Do you want to be a singer because you desire fame, money, and glory? Or did God give you an amazing voice and you love using your gift and sharing it with others?

Selfish motives will make you see other people as something to be used in order to achieve your own goals. Godly motives help you see the value of every human being, whether or not they play a role in your success.

. . . .

Father God, I thank You for giving me my talents.
Reveal to me any selfish motives, and help me value
the gifts of those around me more than my own.

Curb the Complaining

*Do everything without
complaining and arguing.*
PHILIPPIANS 2:14 NLT

Think about the last time you had to do something you really, really didn't want to do. Did you do it joyfully? Or did you complain and grumble the whole time?

Nothing brings down a situation faster than complaining and bickering. In fact, the smallest drop of whining or arguing can poison an entire experience. It throws our attitude into a tailspin of dissatisfaction. The opposite of complaining is gratitude, and a dash of thankfulness can diffuse even the toughest situation.

If you're not careful, complaining can become your default attitude. Try to see every situation as an opportunity to glorify God. By expressing thanks in all things, even if it's not what you want, you'll rip a complaining spirit out by its roots.

· ·

*Lord, please help me do things with joy and
gratitude. I don't want to be a complainer!*

Good for the Soul

Those who are kind benefit themselves,
but the cruel bring ruin on themselves.
PROVERBS 11:17 NIV

We often encourage kindness because it's good for the person receiving it. (Which it is!) However, a kind person also reaps many benefits.

Kindness strengthens friendships, encourages peace, and brings joy to both the giver and receiver. Choosing kindness softens your heart, while meanness hardens it.

An act of kindness is like ripping a weed out of your heart, making room for beautiful things to grow. When you sow kindness, you'll reap peace, joy, and love. If you sow cruelty, you'll reap anger, bitterness, and hatred.

• •

Thank You, Jesus, for all the blessings
You give to those who practice kindness.

Evidence of the Holy Spirit

*But the fruit of the Spirit is love, joy,
peace, patience, kindness, goodness,
faithfulness, gentleness, self-control.*
GALATIANS 5:22–23 NASB

I'm not sure if you've watched any of the dozens of crime dramas currently on TV, but in many episodes there's a court scene where the lawyers present evidence that proves whether someone committed a crime.

In this verse, the apostle Paul gives us a list of evidence to prove whether the Holy Spirit is working in us. Based on this list of character traits, if an objective group of people watched you live your life, would they be convinced the Holy Spirit dwells within you?

. . . .

*Holy Spirit, I invite You to take over my life!
I want to follow Your leading, and I want
Your fruit to be obvious in my life.*

No Law against Kindness

There is no law against these things!
GALATIANS 5:23 NLT

Right before this verse, the apostle Paul listed the fruit of the Spirit: love, joy, peace, patience, kindness, goodness, faithfulness, and self-control. (You can see the previous page for that devotion!)

These fruits mark spiritual maturity. You won't find laws against these character traits anywhere in the Bible. No matter the situation, if you're practicing and growing in these things, you can confidently know you're pleasing God.

Dear heavenly Father, give me opportunities to grow in faith and obedience, and strengthen my confidence that You're pleased with me.

Pray for Your Enemies

"You have heard that it was said, 'You shall love your neighbor and hate your enemy.' But I say to you, love your enemies and pray for those who persecute you."
Matthew 5:43–44 NASB

During His ministry on earth, Jesus took time to correct false teachings that had emerged over the years. In this instance, spiritual leaders had been telling God's people that they had to love their neighbor, but hating their enemy was okay. Jesus corrects this error and raises the bar by telling them something baffling: love your neighbor, but love your enemy also!

Think about someone you'd consider an enemy. If *enemy* is too strong a word, think of a rival or bully. Can you pray sincerely that God blesses and prospers them? When we pray for those who don't treat us nicely, we give them a grace they don't know they're getting.

By blessing your enemy, you surrender to God a burden that will only weigh you down.

• •

Lord, I ask that You bless those who treat me badly. I pray that they will come to know Your loving grace.

Simple Gifts

"He causes his sun to rise on the evil and the good,
and sends rain on the righteous and the unrighteous."
MATTHEW 5:45 NIV

God blesses both the saved and unsaved with common graces. Hope of a new day, seeing the glory of the sun setting behind the mountains, and watching waves crash onto the beach are all simple gifts everyone gets to enjoy.

As a child of God, you have the opportunity to show common grace to those around you. You can extend a smile, give a welcoming hello, share a meal, and offer a listening ear. Through these simple acts, many may come to know Jesus as King. Imagine the joy in knowing they'll receive eternal graces in addition to the temporary ones given in this life.

* *

Father God, teach me to extend
common grace to everyone around me,
especially those who don't know You.

Path of Life

*You will make known to me the path of life;
in Your presence is fullness of joy; in Your
right hand there are pleasures forever.*
PSALM 16:11 NASB

Once, while driving through a small town, I got lost. My phone wouldn't pick up a signal, and I didn't know where I was or which direction to go. I felt overwhelmed and scared. I pulled into a gas station to ask for directions, and a local man overheard me saying I was lost. The road I needed to take was tricky to find, he said. He offered to get in his car and drive in front of me, then honk and point when we approached the turn. He didn't just tell me where to find the road; he *showed* me.

God doesn't just tell us about the path leading to eternal life; He takes our hand and *shows* it to us. Without His help, we'd never see it. He gently guides us to the road that leads to eternal life in His presence.

* * *

*Dear heavenly Father, take me by the hand
and lead me to the path of righteousness!*

Gracious Protection

*Then the LORD God provided a leafy plant and
made it grow up over Jonah to give shade for
his head to ease his discomfort, and Jonah
was very happy about the plant.*
JONAH 4:6 NIV

The story of Jonah gives us a picture of God's over-whelming grace. God instructed Jonah to tell the people of Nineveh to turn from their sin. Rather than obey God's command, Jonah fled. When Jonah finally obeyed, the Ninevites listened, repented, and were spared God's judgment. Jonah was angry because of this, but even then, God provided a plant that grew for his comfort and protection.

The Lord protects us even in our rebellion. This isn't an excuse to keep running from obedience, but an opportunity to praise God for His mercy. If you're en-joying God-given comforts while avoiding what God's calling you to do, don't delay any longer! Listen, obey, and watch God work!

• •

*Dear God, I'm sorry for ignoring Your
voice. I know obedience brings peace and joy.
Help me do what I know You're calling me to do!*

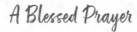

A Blessed Prayer

Now Jabez called on the God of Israel, saying,
"Oh that You would bless me indeed and enlarge
my border, and that Your hand might be with me,
and that You would keep me from harm that it may not
pain me!" And God granted him what he requested.
1 CHRONICLES 4:10 NASB

Have you ever done a genealogy test? The kind where they track where you and your family came from? In the Bible, 1 Chronicles reads like a big family tree. Descendants of Israel are listed, with little or no information given about each person. That changes though, when we get to Jabez. The writer stops to tell us something important about Jabez: he asked something of God, and God gave it to him.

Jabez loved the Lord and trusted God enough to ask for blessings. We serve a God who delights in being asked for things by His children. God will only do what's best for us, which frees us to ask big and leave the outcome in His hands.

* * *

Lord, Your blessings are incredible!
I ask that You always be near, help me
succeed, and protect me from harm.

Asking for Snakes

*"Or which one of you, if his son asks him
for bread, will give him a stone? Or if he asks
for a fish, will give him a serpent? If you then,
who are evil, know how to give good gifts to your
children, how much more will your Father who is in
heaven give good things to those who ask him!"*
MATTHEW 7:9–11 ESV

Recently I visited a friend and watched as she gave her kids things when they asked. She gave them water, snacks, cuddles, and toys. Then her toddler wanted to play with some kitchen knives. She said no, which made him very angry. My friend, being a good mother, didn't give him something he desired, because she knew it would hurt him or others.

Sometimes we ask God for things that might hurt us. We beg for snakes and stones thinking they're bread and fish. God loves us so much that He says no to things that would hurt us. What feels like a punishment is actually God keeping us from getting hurt.

*Lord, help me ask for good things—
and trust You when You say no.*

Leave Grudges Behind

*Make a clean break with all cutting, backbiting,
profane talk. Be gentle with one another,
sensitive. Forgive one another as quickly and
thoroughly as God in Christ forgave you.*
EPHESIANS 4:31–32 MSG

Have you ever done something that you wish you could
go back and undo? Now, what if someone brought up
that "something" every time they saw you? Think of the
shame and embarrassment you'd feel if you were constantly reminded of your mistake.

One of the kindest things you can do for someone
is forgive quickly and not weaponize their past sins—
especially if they're doing their best to learn and grow
from them. We all make mistakes. When someone does
something hurtful, handle it with gentleness, and don't
bring up flaws as a way of punishing them.

*Holy Spirit, please convict me when I'm about
to use the past unfairly against someone.
Help me forgive fully and always be gentle.*

A Soft Answer

A gentle response defuses anger,
but a sharp tongue kindles a temper-fire.
PROVERBS 15:1 MSG

When it comes to handling fire, certain substances will extinguish a flame, while other things will cause it to grow. When it comes to emotions, certain responses will put out anger, while other responses will feed it.

As fires grow, they get even harder to put out. A sarcastic, angry, or passive-aggressive response will only escalate things. A gentle response, however, is like throwing a bucket of cold water on a fire. It'll stall its growth or put it out entirely.

• •

Dear God, I know it's best to always respond
with gentleness, but sometimes it's so hard
not to get defensive. I'm going to work on
extinguishing anger before it spreads.

Cautious Anger

*Be not quick in your spirit to become angry,
for anger lodges in the heart of fools.*
ECCLESIASTES 7:9 ESV

If you want to see the worst of humanity, go to a popular YouTube video and read the comments. They're filled with hurtful, hateful, and angry remarks, often having nothing to do with the video they're under.

We live in a society that's incredibly quick to become angry and offended over the smallest things. It's not enough to quietly dislike or disagree with someone; many people feel the need to completely tear the person down.

Rather than give yourself over to anger, try to become "unoffendable." Be the kind of person others can talk to without fearing an angry outburst or condescending lecture. If you must express an opinion or speak a truth, say it with gentleness and love, listening as much as you talk. (Oh, and try to do it face-to-face, not Snap to Snap. That always goes much better.)

* *

*Dear Jesus, I know it's important to be slow
to anger. Make me someone who stays calm
even when everyone else is worked up.*

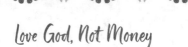

Love God, Not Money

*Don't love money; be satisfied with what
you have. For God has said, "I will never
fail you. I will never abandon you."*
HEBREWS 13:5 NLT

Money can get you a lot in life: comfort, status, education, access to health care, trendy clothes, and lots of material possessions. Money, however, can't buy some of the most important things you need. A large bank account will never heal your broken heart or forgive your sin. It will never bring you peace of mind. (After all, the more you have, the more you have to lose.) Wealth won't give you more friends (at least not true friends), a better attitude, or fulfillment. In fact, a love for money often overshadows a love for kindness.

Don't obsess over getting temporary, perishable things. Instead, develop a love for God, who stores up irreplaceable treasures for you in heaven. Be grateful for the provision God's given you, be it great or small, and give thanks that the most important things you need were given freely on the cross.

• •

*Lord, I know money was given to be used
for Your glory. Help keep me from getting
attached to money and earthly things.*

Set a Good Example

*"See that you do not despise one of these little
ones. For I tell you that in heaven their angels always
see the face of my Father who is in heaven."*
MATTHEW 18:10 ESV

When my sister and I were little, we sold candy bars to raise money for her gymnastics team. Our grandmother owned a hair salon and let us sell the candy to her customers. Some customers bought one; others passed up the opportunity to contribute to such a worthy cause. But one lady bought a ton of candy bars and then *gave them back* to me and my sister so we could eat them. I still remember that woman's generosity decades later. (And my parents still remember the dental bill.)

Your small act of kindness can leave an eternal impact on a child. Whether it's babysitting and playing games, listening to their stories and showing interest in what matters to them, or telling them about Jesus, you have the opportunity to show a child their worth in Christ simply by caring.

- -

*I know children are special to You, Jesus.
Give me opportunities to show kindness
and goodness to kids around me.*

Biblical Revenge

If your enemy is hungry, give him food to eat;
if he is thirsty, give him water to drink. In
doing this, you will heap burning coals on
his head, and the LORD will reward you.
PROVERBS 25:21–22 NIV

Did you know that kindness can be used as a weapon against your enemy? If you want to get revenge on someone who's hurt you, treat them kindly.

Goodness catches wicked people off guard. When someone mistreats you, they expect anger and retaliation. (Two normal responses when hurt.) If that doesn't happen, it confuses them or even angers them. Meeting anger with kindness shows your enemy that their actions didn't shake your foundation.

By offering blessings instead of curses, your enemy sees there's another way. In fact, your generous reaction might even convict them of their sin and make them rethink the path they're on. No matter their response, the Lord will see your obedience and reward you.

* * * * *

Father God, it's so hard to show kindness to the
people who make my life miserable. Give me the
strength to be kind even when I want revenge.

Entertaining Angels

*Do not neglect to show hospitality
to strangers, for by this some have
entertained angels without knowing it.*
HEBREWS 13:2 NASB

Imagine heaven and earth overlapping through your act of kindness. There's so much about the spiritual realm that remains a mystery to us, but throughout the Bible we're told about angels and how they take on many forms.

By showing hospitality to strangers, you might very well be serving angels. It's crazy to think about! Our hearts and motives are put to the test through angels in disguise because, in the words of former publisher Malcom Forbes, "You can easily judge the character of others by how they treat those who can do nothing for them."

• •

Dear God, I can't imagine coming face-to-face with an angel! Through my kindness, I want to be the kind of person who entertains angels without realizing it.

The Good News

And then he told them, "Go into all the world and preach the Good News to everyone."

MARK 16:15 NLT

Every human being is born into this world affected by sin. The good news of the Gospel, however, is that Jesus took care of the penalty for sin when He died on the cross. If you've put your trust in Jesus as your Savior, then you have received healing and are no longer under the curse of sin!

The kindest thing you can do for a person is tell them about this gift. Not everyone will want it, but in sharing that it exists, people who've been searching for hope will find life!

Dear God, I want people to know what Jesus did on the cross for them! Please give me boldness to speak the truth about this good news to everyone.

Take a Rest

*By the seventh day God had finished the work
he had been doing; so on the seventh day he rested
from all his work. Then God blessed the seventh
day and made it holy, because on it he rested
from all the work of creating that he had done.*
GENESIS 2:2–3 NIV

If we're going to be effective workers for the kingdom, we must learn to rest. God set an example for us by resting after six days of creating. As beings created in His image, we're meant to take breaks from our work.

Taking a set time away from your daily routine will revive your spirit and reset your focus. Consider taking a day—or a few hours if a full day is impossible—to take a break from "life." This might require a little bit of advanced planning if you need to get ahead with homework or do some chores, but when you commit to resting your body and mind every now and then, you'll be better equipped to make kind choices.

*Dear Lord, I know rest is important. Give me
opportunities to rest and restore my soul!*

Known by Our Love

"By this all people will know that you are my disciples, if you have love for one another."
JOHN 13:35 ESV

If you follow Jesus, then you're an ambassador for God's kingdom. You represent Christ here on earth. When people look at you, they get a glimpse of Jesus.

As a Christ follower, your life will look different. One of the biggest things people notice is how Christians treat other people. Complaining, gossiping, and holding grudges are typical behaviors of the world. Instead, love, serve, and speak well of all people, but especially your brothers and sisters in Christ. Build them up and encourage them. By this the world will look and say, "Oh, that's unique!"

• •

Dear God, help me love my brothers and sisters in Christ in such a way that the world knows my devotion to You!

Take Your Worries to Jesus

*Then Jesus said, "Come to me, all of
you who are weary and carry heavy
burdens, and I will give you rest."*
MATTHEW 11:28 NLT

Let's face it: sometimes life gets incredibly hard. If
you're overwhelmed by the heaviness of the world, then
run, limp, or crawl as fast as you can into the arms of
Jesus!

True rest is found in the arms of the Savior, who
loves you and holds you close during the worst moments of your life. He'll restore your confidence and
remind you of your worth.

When you feel like you can't go on, the Author and
Perfecter of your faith draws you close to Him, reminding you that you're loved, protected, and cherished.

• •

*Dear heavenly Father, sometimes life gets
really discouraging and it's hard to find any
hope. I want You to take my hurts and fears
and replace them with purpose and peace.*

Endless Distractions

*Make the most of every
opportunity in these evil days.*
EPHESIANS 5:16 NLT

Have you ever opened up YouTube or Instagram and thought, *I'll just watch one video*, or *I'll scroll real quick and then get going*, and then, before you knew it, two hours had passed?

We live in an era of endless distractions. Hundreds of apps, TV networks, and companies compete for our time, attention, and clicks. Many of these things are okay in moderation, but often they consume so much of our time that we miss out on opportunities to serve, connect, and enjoy the world around us.

Be aware of your screen time. You only get one shot at today. Will you spend it looking at a device, or will you spend it looking for opportunities to be a different kind of light in a world lit by screens?

• •

Dear Jesus, I confess that I don't always manage my time in a way that honors You. Help me use technology wisely so that I don't miss opportunities for kindness.

God Redeems Evil

"Don't you see, you planned evil against me but God used those same plans for my good, as you see all around you right now—life for many people."
GENESIS 50:20 MSG

At the end of Genesis, we're told the story of Joseph. Joseph was betrayed by his brothers, sold into slavery, falsely accused of a crime, and then thrown into prison. He had every reason to be angry and bitter. Yet the Bible tells us he forgave those who hurt him.

Joseph knew God's plan for good overruled his brothers' plan for evil. Joseph ended up in a position of power in Egypt, and his wisdom helped save countless people from starvation during a famine. Joseph realized God used every injustice for His sovereign and good purposes.

. . . .

There's so much evil in the world, Lord God. When things seem hopeless, help me remember that You're working everything for good.

Bless the Lord

*Bless the LORD, O my soul, and all
that is within me, bless his holy name!*
PSALM 103:1 ESV

How does a simple human bless God?

We bless the Lord with shouts of praise, confessions of sin, and humble hearts. We bless Him through joyful obedience and with acts of kindness. We bless Him by growing in our knowledge of Him so we can praise Him even more.

The Lord has done more for you than your mind can fathom. Praise Him and bless Him with all that is in you!

• •

*Dear almighty God, You're magnificent, holy,
and worthy of all our praise. I thank You and
praise You for everything You've done.*

Overcome Evil with Good

Do not be overcome by evil,
but overcome evil with good.
ROMANS 12:21 NASB

Hearing bad news or seeing a story about something tragic can quickly send us spiraling into a state of fear and panic. Sometimes it feels like the world is overrun by sadness, and it's easy to become overwhelmed by the presence of hardship. Before you fall into complete despair though, look at the tools God's given you to fight evil: goodness, kindness, prayer, and love.

Your commitment to kindness brings light into the darkness. Darkness can't exist where the light shines because the light overpowers it. An act of kindness is a sign to the world that hope exists.

* * * * *

Father God, let Your light shine through the
darkness! Give me opportunities to fight evil
with my attitude and actions. I want to live
a life of love, kindness, and goodness.

Fiery Anger

And don't stay angry. Don't go to bed angry.
Don't give the Devil that kind of foothold in your life.
Ephesians 4:26–27 msg

Did you know that if a building catches on fire, the fire spreads slower if all the doors inside are closed? Open doors allow the fire easy access into all areas of the structure.

Staying angry is like leaving doors open for temptation and sin to enter freely. When anger is present, retaliation, hatred, and bitterness are never far behind.

If we close the door to anger, the temptation to sin won't spread into our lives as quickly. It might hover outside the door, but it'll give us fair warning of its presence, allowing us time to plan our escape.

Sometimes I can't find the "off switch" to
my anger, God. Please give me the ability
to close the door on my anger today!

Blessed Loyalty

But Ruth said, "Do not urge me to leave you or to return from following you. For where you go I will go, and where you lodge I will lodge. Your people shall be my people, and your God my God."

RUTH 1:16 ESV

The book of Ruth tells us the story of Ruth (not too surprising) and her mother-in-law, Naomi. After Ruth's husband died, she was free to go back to her family, remarry, and live her own life. Ruth wasn't an Israelite like Naomi, and staying with her meant continuing into a foreign land and unknown circumstances.

Instead of leaving though, Ruth stayed with Naomi. Even though Ruth and Naomi differed in many ways, Ruth trusted God and wanted to stay with His people. Because of her loyalty to God and His people, Ruth ended up marrying an Israelite named Boaz, and she became an ancestor of Jesus.

* * *

Dear God, make me someone who's loyal to You and Your people, even if it means venturing into unknown territory.

God's Precious Love

How precious is Your lovingkindness, O God!
And the children of men take refuge
in the shadow of Your wings.
<small>PSALM 36:7 NASB</small>

Did you know that an eagle's wingspan can reach upward of eight feet long? That means, when an eagle fully stretches its wings, it's taller than most professional basketball players.

Eagles don't just use their wings for flying. They also use them to provide protection to their young. The mama eagle spreads her wings over her young to shield them from snow, rain, and predators.

In His precious loving-kindness, God has enveloped you, His daughter, in the shadow of His wings.

. . . .

Dear heavenly Father, You are my
only true source of refuge. Shelter
me in the shadow of Your wings.

Outside the Comfort Zone

*"Which of these three do you think was a neighbor
to the man who fell into the hands of robbers?" The
expert in the law replied, "The one who had mercy
on him." Jesus told him, "Go and do likewise."*
LUKE 10:36–37 NIV

Sometimes people look for excuses to get out of things
they know they're supposed to do, which is what the experts in the Law were doing here.

They'd just asked Jesus, "Who is my neighbor?"
hoping He'd tell them their neighbors were friends and
family. They didn't want to leave their comfort zone in
order to fulfill God's command to love thy neighbor.

Instead, Jesus told them about the Good Samaritan,
a social outcast who showed compassion to a stranger
in need. Jesus wants us to be a neighbor to everyone
and show mercy to anyone in need, not just to family
and friends.

. . . .

*Dear Jesus, I know it's important to step outside
my comfort zone and show mercy to those in
need. Make me a good neighbor to everyone,
not just those I feel comfortable around.*

Rejoice in Discipline

"For the LORD disciplines those he loves,
and he punishes each one he accepts as his child."
HEBREWS 12:6 NLT

If you've faced the consequences for something you've done wrong, then rejoice! This means the Lord has adopted you as His daughter and is keeping you on the path of righteousness.

Praise God and thank Him for loving you enough to correct you. After all, what good parent lets a child continue in destructive behavior? A good mother or father won't allow their child to keep playing in the street when cars are coming, even if that child wants nothing more than to stay in the street.

Discipline doesn't always feel loving at the time, but God sees the bigger picture and allows a little bit of temporary discomfort to save His children from eternal agony.

- -

Dear God, it's hard to be thankful for discipline,
but I'm grateful You love me enough to reveal
and punish my sins. Help me learn from Your
discipline and stay on the right path.

Wait Quietly

It is good that one should wait
quietly for the salvation of the LORD.
LAMENTATIONS 3:26 ESV

When you feel like God is distant, wait quietly.

When you feel like God doesn't hear you, wait quietly.

When you feel like God has forgotten you, wait quietly.

Wait quietly, resting in the knowledge that God is always near.

Wait quietly, trusting that God's timing is perfect.

Wait quietly, knowing that silence doesn't mean God has forgotten you.

Wait quietly, for the Lord is perfecting the salvation He planned for you before the foundation of the world.

* * *

Lord, help me wait quietly and trust
that Your timing is perfect.

Cruel Words

"I am surrounded by mockers.
I watch how bitterly they taunt me."
JOB 17:2 NLT

There's an old-fashioned saying that goes like this: "Sticks and stones may break my bones, but words will never hurt me."

I've often wondered if the person who coined that phrase ever had cruel words spoken to them. Unkind words hurt deeply, whether they're said directly to our face, told behind our back, or discovered by accident on social media.

When people's words threaten to tear you down, remember who you are in Christ. Lift your head high and know that God says you're loved, redeemed, and cherished.

. . . .

Dear Jesus, cruel words hurt a lot. I'm so glad that
Your words are always true, loving, and life-giving.

The Ultimate Kindness

"For God so loved the world, that He gave His only begotten Son, that whoever believes in Him shall not perish, but have eternal life."
JOHN 3:16 NASB

Our limited human brain will never fully grasp the splendor and majesty of our perfect, eternal, and holy God. Similarly, we'll never completely wrap our minds around how serious, revolting, and hurtful our sins are to God.

When sin entered the world, God could've removed Himself and left humanity to suffer alone. But God loved the world so much that He gave His only Son to take the punishment we deserved so we could be restored to right standing with Him.

When we understand the holiness of God and the horror of sin, we see the incredible mercy, compassion, and kindness shown to us in what Jesus did on the cross. What's more, God made this ultimate kindness open to all who confess their sin and claim Jesus as their Savior.

* * *

Thank You for sending Your Son to take the punishment for our sins, God! What an incredible gift You've given the world.

The Thief on the Cross

Then he said, "Jesus, remember me when you
enter your kingdom." He said, "Don't worry,
I will. Today you will join me in paradise."
LUKE 23:42–43 MSG

As Jesus hung on the cross, life slowly fading from Him, two thieves hung beside Him. One thief mocked Jesus, but the second thief realized he was hanging next to the Son of God and asked to be remembered in Jesus' kingdom.

Jesus promised the second thief that he'd see Him in paradise that same day. What comfort that must've brought to the thief as he took his final breaths!

Even while dying for the sins of humankind, Jesus showed mercy and kindness. The reason Jesus hung on the cross was for people just like the thief. By offering mercy to a dying common criminal, Jesus showed us it's never too late to realize He is King and accept the forgiveness He offers.

Dear Jesus, You are the Son of God and the only One
who can forgive my sins. Thank You for what You did
on the cross, and for Your mercy and kindness to all.

The Last Shall Be First

> *"But many who are the greatest now will be
> least important then, and those who seem
> least important now will be the greatest then."*
> MATTHEW 19:30 NLT

Not too long ago, *Time* magazine put Selena Gomez on their cover as one of the top women changing the world. Her big accomplishment? Being the first person to reach one hundred million followers on Instagram.

We live in a culture that values popularity above all else. "Important" people are the ones getting the most likes and follows. In fact, many of us gauge our own worth by our online popularity. When something we post gets a big response, we feel validated and important. When no one comments or double taps, we become insecure and embarrassed. We look at other people's profiles and compare our importance.

God doesn't care about our likes, follows, and retweets. He wants to see us growing in faith, hope, and love. Our importance in the kingdom of heaven won't be based on follows, but on the One we follow.

. . . .

*Dear God, it's so easy to get consumed with
popularity and the desire to be important.
I need to focus on what matters in eternity.*

The Gift of Faith

But a poor widow came and put in two very small copper coins, worth only a few cents. Calling his disciples to him, Jesus said, "Truly I tell you, this poor widow has put more into the treasury than all the others. They all gave out of their wealth; but she, out of her poverty, put in everything—all she had to live on."
MARK 12:42–44 NIV

One of the greatest gifts you can give to God is your faith. Two small coins might not seem like much, but the faith of a person who entrusts all they have to the Lord can make a big impact for the kingdom of God.

You may not think you have much to offer God, but it doesn't take lots of money or talent to serve Him. God can do more with a humble heart that says, "This is what I have, Lord; it's Yours," than He can with someone who has a million dollars and a hard heart.

. . . .

Dear Jesus, everything I have belongs to You! Give me opportunities to glorify You with the gifts You've given me, even if they seem small to the world.

Renewed Mercies

*The faithful love of the LORD never ends! His
mercies never cease. Great is his faithfulness;
his mercies begin afresh each morning.*
LAMENTATIONS 3:22–23 NLT

If you're like me, you probably have days when you feel
like you're failing at life. You can't handle the stress
of school, you knock over everything you touch, and
instead of extending kindness, you respond angrily
over something small.

If you're discouraged, take heart! When you go
to sleep at night, the Lord continues working in your
heart. Come morning, He presents you with a brand-
new day filled with fresh opportunities for love, kindness, and grace.

No matter how today went, no matter how far you
fell short, tomorrow is a new day. The Lord's mercies are
already there waiting for you.

. . . .

*I can't believe how much I fail sometimes,
Lord Jesus. It's like I can't get anything right.
Help me see Your daily mercies and remember
that You're faithful even when I fail.*

East to West

*As far as the east is from the west, so far has
He removed our transgressions from us.*
PSALM 103:12 NASB

If you're traveling west, you can't be going east at the same time. You'll continue moving west until you switch directions. East and west will never touch each other.

If your hope is in Jesus, then God has completely removed your sins and taken them to a place where they can't haunt you with shame, guilt, and regret.

Not only are your sins forgiven and removed from you, but they also continue moving away as the Lord leads you westward into His waiting salvation.

. . . .

*Dear God, You've shown me such incredible mercy
by taking my sins and removing them completely.
Help me move forward and rest in Your forgiveness.*

Imprisoned for the Gospel

Remember the prisoners, as though in prison
with them, and those who are ill-treated,
since you yourselves also are in the body.
HEBREWS 13:3 NASB

Consider the human body for a moment. When one part of your body hurts—even something as small as a stubbed little toe—your whole body is aware of it.

All around the world, members of Christ's body are mistreated or imprisoned for following Him. We're given two powerful weapons to help our persecuted brothers and sisters: prayer and encouragement. We can take hurting believers in prayer before God and ask Him to rescue them. In some cases, we can send letters of encouragement to those imprisoned and remind them that they're loved and not forgotten.

- -

Dear Lord, comfort and help those suffering
for Your name, and free those imprisoned
because of their belief in You.

All Things for Good

And we know that for those who love God
all things work together for good, for those
who are called according to his purpose.
ROMANS 8:28 ESV

For unbelievers, bad circumstances are simply bad circumstances. When you follow Christ, however, life's difficulties become an opportunity for God to display His power and faithfulness.

What Satan uses to try to destroy your faith, God spins into spiritual gold. He uses hardships to perfect your faith, grow your character, and strengthen your foundation so your hope lies in Him and not in the things of the world.

• •

Dear God, You know that life brings a lot of ups
and downs. It's a gift to know that even the bad
things are worked for my good. Help me trust You
and remember this promise when things get tough.

Alive with Christ

*You were dead because of your sins and because
your sinful nature was not yet cut away. Then God
made you alive with Christ, for he forgave all our sins.*
COLOSSIANS 2:13 NLT

A dead person has no power to change their circumstances. They stay dead unless someone or something brings them to life. (In Disney movies, it's usually the kiss of a prince.)

We're all born dead in our sins. It takes a powerful outside force to cut away our sinful chains, freeing us so we can live. When you put your hope in Jesus, you're made spiritually alive and released from the shackles of sin and sent out to live for Christ.

If your sins have been cut away, you're spiritually free! Now go and live as one who's been given life!

• •

*Dear Jesus, I'm so glad You made me
spiritually alive and cut away the chains of
my sins! I want to honor You with my life and
live as someone who's been given freedom.*

The Promise of a Savior

*GOD told the serpent: "Because you've done this,
you're cursed, cursed beyond all cattle and wild
animals, cursed to slink on your belly and eat dirt
all your life. I'm declaring war between you and
the Woman, between your offspring and hers.
He'll wound your head, you'll wound his heel."*
GENESIS 3:14–15 MSG

These verses may seem a little confusing, but it's the very first time God announces His plan to provide a Savior for humankind. God promises the offspring (Jesus) will wound the head of the enemy (Satan).

After removing Adam and Eve from the garden of Eden, God gave them (and all of humanity!) the hope of salvation. Despite their rebellion, God extended great compassion and mercy to them by giving them the promise of redemption.

Wow. Your plan for salvation has been in place since the beginning, Father God! Thank You for providing me with hope and for giving me a second chance at life.

Kindness to Animals

The righteous care for the needs of their animals,
but the kindest acts of the wicked are cruel.
PROVERBS 12:10 NIV

When God created the world, He placed all of creation under the care of humans. This privilege, however, comes with responsibility. Unnecessary cruelty toward living things shows a disregard for the duty we've been given.

Taking good care of your pets or other animals in your home shows you understand the responsibility given to you as someone bearing the image of God.

. . . .

Heavenly Father, I know You created all things and
placed humans in charge. We abuse this privilege
so often. I want to take responsibility for taking
care of creation and animals.

God Loves the Nations

*"And through your descendants all the
nations of the earth will be blessed—
all because you have obeyed me."*
GENESIS 22:18 NLT

Throughout the Old Testament, God reminds humanity of His promise to bring a Savior. God says over and over that this salvation isn't reserved for a certain country or people group; it's meant for everyone in the entire world!

Even though God used the lineage of Israel to bring Jesus to earth, He did it to bless all nations. Every culture, tribe, tongue, and people would receive the gift of salvation brought forth through His chosen people.

It's important to remember and support our Christian brothers and sisters around the world. Even though we may look different and our cultures sometimes have little in common, the blood of Christ makes us one family.

*Lord, strengthen Your Church around the world!
Bring people from all over the globe to faith in You.*

Action!

*They claim to know God, but by their
actions they deny him. They are detestable,
disobedient and unfit for doing anything good.*
TITUS 1:16 NIV

What do your actions say about your belief in God? Do you tell people you follow Jesus and then turn around and do things that hurt your witness? If you're claiming Jesus as your Savior, the world is watching to see if your life matches what you say.

As you walk with Jesus, you'll grow in your desire to serve Him with both your attitude and actions. If you have no desire to honor God in the way you live your life, ask yourself this question: "Do I actually *know* Jesus, or do I only know *about* Him?"

* * *

*Dear Jesus, change my heart so that
I love Your commands. I don't want
to deny You with my actions!*

Holy Wardrobe

I delight greatly in the LORD; my soul rejoices in my
God. For he has clothed me with garments of salvation
and arrayed me in a robe of his righteousness. . .
as a bride adorns herself with her jewels.
ISAIAH 61:10 NIV

During award-show season, actresses take great care in picking the perfect dress and accessories to wear to each event. (Guys have it much easier with tuxes.) Reporters always ask the same question to nominees as they walk the red carpet: "Who are you wearing?" The dress's designer says a lot about the importance of the person wearing it.

God has designed special garments for His children that reveal our importance. He dresses us as royalty, starting with robes of righteousness, which show that we're redeemed and cleansed from all sin. He spares no expense in adorning us in the finest jewelry, so everyone knows we're valued, worthy, and cherished in the presence of our Savior.

* * * * *

It's so easy to feel unimportant and overlooked,
Lord. Remind me of who I am in You, and
help me wear with confidence the amazing
spiritual clothes You've made for me!

Cheap Imitation Faith

Count it all joy, my brothers, when you meet trials
of various kinds, for you know that the testing
of your faith produces steadfastness. And let
steadfastness have its full effect, that you may
be perfect and complete, lacking in nothing.
JAMES 1:2–4 ESV

Growing up, my mom never let me get cheap earrings. Instead, she'd make me wait. Then, for my birthday or Christmas, she'd buy me nice earrings made from high-quality materials that wouldn't irritate my skin or break. She gave me the real thing and not a poorly made imitation.

God loves us so much that He doesn't let us settle for a cheap imitation faith. Just as the gold used to make expensive jewelry is put into a fire to remove damaging impurities, God tests our faith with trials, leaving a pure, strong, and precious faith that will last into eternity.

I don't want cheap, substitute faith, Father God.
Teach me to have joy in my trials, knowing
You're using them to strengthen my faith.

Cross-Training

*Practice these things, immerse yourself in
them, so that all may see your progress.*
1 TIMOTHY 4:15 ESV

Good athletes do something called cross-training,
where they practice different sports or exercises to tar-
get muscles not worked in their everyday routines. By
mixing up their training regimen, they're more well
rounded and prepared for competition.

Working on other character traits like generosity,
mercy, patience, and self-control strengthens your ability to choose kindness. Aim to become well rounded
in your faith, exercising every spiritual muscle as you
grow in the Lord. Show the world that, with God, kindness is always possible.

- -

*Dear God, I want to be a good spiritual athlete,
strong in character and faith. Help me practice
kindness, generosity, and self-control.*

The Gift of Peace

*The things you have learned and received and
heard and seen in me, practice these things,
and the God of peace will be with you.*
PHILIPPIANS 4:9 NASB

When a "mean girl" kept teasing Mariah in class, she
simply dealt with it quietly. One day, Mariah thought
of the perfect comeback. She imagined the satisfaction
she'd feel putting this bully in her place.

A couple days later, when the girl began picking on
her again, Mariah pulled out her response. It worked.
The girl left her alone and even retreated to the back
of the class, not saying anything else the whole period.
Mariah felt satisfied at first, but as the day went on,
she began feeling guilty. "I thought getting back at her
would make me feel better," she mused.

Sometimes vengeance feels good in the moment,
but later we feel bad knowing we've caused the same
pain to others that was caused to us. Practicing kindness, even when revenge makes more sense, leaves
us with an even better gift: the peace of our heavenly
Father.

. . . .

*Dear Jesus, I want to act kindly in unjust
situations. Give me Your peace, Lord!*

A No-Bragging Policy

For by grace you have been saved through faith;
and that not of yourselves, it is the gift of God;
not as a result of works, so that no one may boast.
EPHESIANS 2:8–9 NASB

"I'm not *that* bad!" you might say to yourself when someone tells you that you're a sinner. Even the best of us have sinned at least once, and a perfect, holy God can't associate with even the tiniest sin. If the smallest speck gets on a pure white cloth, it's no longer pure white. It's been tainted.

Fortunately, God provided a way for us to be made clean through the sacrifice of Jesus. What's free to us cost God everything. Jesus never sinned but suffered a sinner's death on our behalf.

The Gospel leaves zero room for bragging. Receive it with humility, and let the magnitude of this great gift you've been given motivate you to good works.

. . . .

Lord Jesus, reveal to me the depths of my sin and
rebellion. Thank You for giving up everything
so that I can have a relationship with You.

Focus Up

Set your minds on things above,
not on earthly things.
COLOSSIANS 3:2 NIV

"Don't forget, look up at me!" the choir director told her singers. "Otherwise, you'll miss the cutoff for that last note."

Most of the choir followed their director's instruction, but as the song neared its end, Sarah got distracted by a stain on a nearby soprano's shirt. Was it mustard? Some kind of jelly? Suddenly, Sarah realized her voice was the only one singing. She'd forgotten to look up and missed the cutoff!

If you're going to live a life of kindness, you'll need to continually look up and follow the One who's orchestrating the entire universe from His heavenly throne. You must focus your mind on things above. Don't get so caught up in the petty things happening here on earth that you miss what He's calling you to do.

Dear heavenly Father, I really need to focus on
You and not the things of this world. Help me
remember to "look up" and obey Your commands.

Cast Your Anxieties on the Lord

*Cast all your anxiety on him
because he cares for you.*
1 PETER 5:7 NIV

"Live one day at a time." "Just take deep breaths." "Don't worry, it'll all work out." People often use one of these phrases to make us feel better when we're anxious or worried. The world can be a scary place, and trying to predict what the future holds can make the calmest person go crazy.

God invites you to cast, throw, and fling your troubles onto His back. He *wants* you to burden Him with your anxieties. He cares for you and doesn't want you shouldering heavy burdens, especially when He's willing and able to carry them for you.

• •

*Take my anxiety and worry, Lord God! It's too
much for me to carry! Please bring the right
people into my life who can help me handle
my fears when they get out of control.*

Image Bearers

God created man in His own image,
in the image of God He created him;
male and female He created them.

<small>GENESIS 1:27 NASB</small>

If you look into a mirror, you'll see your reflection. The reflection isn't actually you, but it shows your features to the real you.

God made humans in His own image. We don't necessarily physically look like God, but we possess many of His character traits. Our ability to love, have relationships, work, and create are all qualities that reflect our Creator.

Every person you meet bears the image of God. By showing kindness, you're honoring God and telling the world they're valued by their Creator.

. . . .

Dear God, it's hard to wrap my mind around the
fact that I reflect You. Help me bear Your image
well and treat other image bearers with kindness.

Stop, Drop, and Listen

Understand this, my dear brothers and sisters: You must all be quick to listen, slow to speak, and slow to get angry.
JAMES 1:19 NLT

One of the most powerful gifts you can give to a friend is your full attention when they have something to say. Don't try to fix the problem, don't interrupt them, and don't get angry if they say something you disagree with.

Instead, stop what you're doing, drop the phone, and *listen*. Listen to *know* what they're going through. Listen to *understand* their heart. Listen to *care* for their soul.

Listening helps carry their burden because they know someone else understands what they're going through. Listening also communicates a very powerful message. It says, "What you're going through matters to me. Even more importantly, what you're going through matters to God."

· ·

Dear heavenly Father, make me a good listener. Help me be the kind of friend who listens more than speaks.

The Point of Kindness

*Don't you see how wonderfully kind, tolerant,
and patient God is with you? Does this mean
nothing to you? Can't you see that his kindness
is intended to turn you from your sin?*

ROMANS 2:4 NLT

The purpose of God's kindness is to turn you away from your sins. If you say, "Thank You, God, for forgiving my sins!" in one breath, and in the very next go and sin again on purpose, you're taking advantage of God's grace.

When you're tempted to sin, remember what a patient, kind, and loving Savior you serve. Run away from temptation and into the arms of Jesus!

*Dear God, I want to run away from my
sins and toward You. Thank You for Your
patience and kindness toward me.*

The Need to Be Right

A fool takes no pleasure in understanding,
but only in expressing his opinion.
PROVERBS 18:2 ESV

Some people love to talk and take great pleasure in always saying what's on their mind. They have no desire to hear other opinions; they just want the world to know what they think about something. The Bible calls these people fools.

There's a time and a place to speak up, but a wise person knows that listening is better than being heard. By giving someone the chance to speak, we show them they're more important than our need to be right.

. . . .

I know I need to surrender my need to be right.
Holy Spirit, give me the wisdom to know
when to speak and when to be quiet.

Restful Places

He makes me lie down in green pastures;
He leads me beside quiet waters.
PSALM 23:2 NASB

I've never met a toddler that voluntarily goes down for a nap. (Though I'm sure one exists somewhere.) Most young children view rest as an interruption to their playtime agenda. A good parent, however, makes their child lie down in a place where they can rest, knowing their son or daughter will enjoy the remaining hours of the day with a more joyful attitude after some sleep.

Sometimes God *makes* His children lie down in calm, peaceful places because He knows they need a break. Seasons when things "just aren't happening" might be God giving you space for rest. God may force you away from your full schedule in order to restore your soul. Once restored, you can set out on the mission He's put before you.

• •

Lead me to quiet waters, Lord! Help me not
to resist when You're telling me it's time to rest.

Gentle Power

Through patience a ruler can be persuaded,
and a gentle tongue can break a bone.
PROVERBS 25:15 NIV

Careless talk is the equivalent of lifting one-pound weights. It takes almost no effort, and pretty much anyone can do it without trying. Calm, grace-filled speech, on the other hand, takes Olympian-level strength.

God can use our careful, gentle words to break down the strongest barriers and touch even the most hurting, calloused hearts.

* * *

Dear Lord, I want my speech to be gentle
and thoughtful. Give me the self-control
to use my words carefully.

God Chooses the Weak

But God chose the foolish things of the world
to shame the wise; God chose the weak
things of the world to shame the strong.
1 CORINTHIANS 1:27 NIV

Do you feel weak or inadequate? Then rejoice! God has handpicked you to be strong in Him!

Do you struggle in school and worry you're not smart enough? Be at peace, for the Holy Spirit doesn't require high test scores to fill you with wisdom!

Do you watch as everyone around you gets picked and awarded and celebrated, and wonder, *Will I ever get noticed?* Take heart, because Jesus picked you to be His daughter and delights in everything about you.

The wisdom of God shames what the world deems important. While the world screams, "Power! Riches! Fame! Beauty!" God says, "Love! Humility! Kindness! Sacrifice!" The Lord takes great pleasure in using people the world sees as unimportant or unfit to do incredible things for His kingdom.

• •

Dear God, show Your great power through my weakness.
Teach me to value what's important to You and not
become consumed with what the world values.

Valuing the Church

Therefore, whenever we have the opportunity,
we should do good to everyone—especially
to those in the family of faith.
GALATIANS 6:10 NLT

As you go through life, you'll have many opportunities to do good. You should always jump at the chance to help someone—especially other believers. As needs arise, don't hesitate to show your brothers and sisters in Christ that they're valued members of your family.

If you're not already part of a church or plugged into a youth group, consider making that a priority. No one understands the challenges of living for God better than other followers of Christ. You'll need their support as you continue striving to live a life marked by obedience and kindness.

. . . .

Dear God, thank You for giving me such an
amazing extended spiritual family. Help me
eagerly take care of those in Your body.

Have Your Plank Removed

"Why do you look at the speck that is in your brother's eye, but do not notice the log that is in your own eye?"
MATTHEW 7:3 NASB

"Kelly is the worst. All she does is complain, complain, complain. Does she even hear herself? It's so annoying," Hannah complained to her friend.

See the irony?

It's incredibly easy to notice when someone else does something wrong. It's much, much harder to notice your own shortcomings. Before you start correcting others or gossiping about their failures to your friends, ask yourself this question: "What's my plank?"

If you're not sure, ask a close friend or family member where they think you can improve. It's humbling to hear what they have to say, but once your plank is removed, you'll see clearer than before. Plus, you'll be so busy noticing mountains and flowers and other beautiful things you missed when the plank blocked your vision, you'll barely notice any specks!

• •

Holy Spirit, reveal to me what my plank is, even if it hurts my pride. Help me be gracious to others and keep my focus on how I can improve my own shortcomings.

The Kindness of Honesty

Faithful are the wounds of a friend,
but deceitful are the kisses of an enemy.
PROVERBS 27:6 NASB

A true friend tells you what you *need* to hear, not what you *want* to hear.

Only an enemy lets someone continue on a path leading to destruction. An enemy will use flattery to encourage sin if it helps them achieve their own goals.

Sometimes the kindest thing you can do for someone is tell them the truth. If you notice sinful patterns and destructive habits, it might be time to gently and lovingly talk to your friend about what you've noticed. They might feel offended at the time, but a small wound now may save them from a world of hurt later.

• •

Dear God, I want to be a good friend, the kind who speaks the truth in love, even when it might hurt. Help make my words gentle and kind, and bring growth in both me and my friends in tough situations.

Keep Your Friend's Confidence

*A gossip goes around telling secrets, but those
who are trustworthy can keep a confidence.*
PROVERBS 11:13 NLT

The fastest way to destroy a friendship is to share a secret that doesn't belong to you.

It might make you feel good to have some inside scoop on a particular situation, but destroying your friend's confidence will crack the foundation of your friendship. Trust takes a long time to earn and a moment to lose.

A kind friend keeps their mouth shut when a friend confides a secret. The only exception to breaking a confidence is if a friend reveals they're being harmed or harming themselves in some way, in which case what's best for your friend is to share their secret with an adult who has the ability to help them.

. . . .

*Dear Jesus, make me a trustworthy friend.
I want to be the kind of person who can keep
secrets and not destroy friendships with gossip.*

Character-Driven Hope

Not only so, but we also glory in our sufferings,
because we know that suffering produces perseverance;
perseverance, character; and character, hope.
ROMANS 5:3–4 NIV

The world isn't always a kind place. Your life will be marked by trials, both small and big. I'm willing to bet that you've already had to deal with a variety of problems in your life so far.

Every trial you go through shapes you more like Christ. Suffering strengthens your character and tests your faith. As you persevere through all circumstances, you'll discover a deep, lasting sense of hope. This kind of hope isn't dependent on your situation but is firmly rooted in your relationship with Jesus.

• •

Dear Jesus, I ask that You give me a kingdom-minded
attitude about suffering. I know that my trials aren't
a punishment but an opportunity for You to
change me from the inside out.

Healthy Spiritual Competition

Love one another with brotherly affection.
Outdo one another in showing honor.
ROMANS 12:10 ESV

When it comes to showing love to others, we're allowed to be competitive. Make it your goal to outdo everyone else in good deeds. Think of how different the world would be if everyone prioritized the well-being of others over their own desires.

Take a moment now to think of some creative things you can do to make the people around you feel valued today.

. . . .

Dear heavenly Father, I want to be the kind of person who always jumps at opportunities to show honor to my friends, family, and even total strangers. Open my eyes to ways that I can affirm and encourage other people.

Seek a Pure Heart

*One who loves a pure heart and who speaks
with grace will have the king for a friend.*
PROVERBS 22:11 NIV

We don't always love the things we're supposed to love. Sometimes we love being part of a clique more than we love being kind and friendly to everyone. Sometimes we love binge-watching morally questionable shows or playing video games more than we love studying God's Word or being productive with our time. We must learn to love what's pure. Remember. . .

A pure heart doesn't seek its own gain but does what's right in each situation.

A pure heart speaks with grace, knowing words contain the power to heal or destroy.

A pure heart longs for what God values and not what the world says is important.

A pure heart is rare in this world and important; people are refreshed by the friendship of someone possessing this unique gift.

. . . .

*I don't always desire what a pure heart desires,
Father God. Help me learn to love what's
pure moment by moment, day by day.*

Loving God and People

*If anyone boasts, "I love God," and goes right on
hating his brother or sister, thinking nothing of it,
he is a liar. If he won't love the person he can see,
how can he love the God he can't see? The command
we have from Christ is blunt: Loving God includes
loving people. You've got to love both.*

1 JOHN 4:20–21 MSG

The way you treat other people supports or denies your claim to love God. After all, it's easy to *say* you love God, but the *proof* that you love God lies in how you act toward those around you.

You can't love God without loving people. If you claim to love God but belittle, hate, and seek revenge against other people, you're denying what you believe with your behavior.

People who love God do their best to love their neighbor. They practice kindness, generosity, and self-lessness, knowing that through these actions their love for God will be spoken loudly to the world.

. . . .

*I love You, God, and I want the world
to know by my actions that I love You.
Make me a good witness in all I say and do.*

Angry People

*Don't hang out with angry people; don't keep
company with hotheads. Bad temper is
contagious—don't get infected.*
PROVERBS 22:24–25 MSG

How does a person show kindness in an increasingly angry and hot-tempered society? By not becoming angry and hot tempered.

Sometimes the best way to love an angry person is to keep them at a distance. We're called to love everyone, but that doesn't necessarily mean you must invite a hot-tempered person into your inner circle of friends. Bad attitudes are contagious and hard to get rid of once there.

Instead, pray for people you know who've given their lives over to anger. Pray that God will protect you from anger and give you the strength to show gentleness and peace when you're in the company of angry, bitter people.

• •

*Dear Lord, give me wisdom in who I spend my
time with. I know that the people closest to me will
influence me the most. Bring me friends who love You
and will encourage me to live a life honoring You.*

Friend and Intercessor

*"My intercessor is my friend as my eyes pour
out tears to God; on behalf of a man he pleads
with God as one pleads for a friend."*
JOB 16:20–21 NIV

Life, dear sister, will contain seasons of unimaginable sadness, heartache, and loneliness.

In these times, remember that you have a Friend and Intercessor in the heavens, mediating on your behalf. An intercessor goes before God to plead your case and call for action. Jesus, the best friend you could ever have, takes your prayers, hurts, and tears directly before the throne of God.

Jesus has a special connection with those suffering. He lived and walked on this earth and experienced hurt, sorrow, and betrayal. Because Jesus is fully God, He knows what's best for you and can see the outcome of your trials. Because He is fully human, He can comfort and sustain you through the storms.

. . . .

*Thank You, Lord Jesus, for interceding on my behalf.
Life hurts, and sometimes I feel so hopeless and lost.
Comfort me and give me hope, Jesus, as only You can.*

Surrendering Vengeance

*"May the LORD judge between you and me.
And may the LORD avenge the wrongs you have
done to me, but my hand will not touch you.
As the old saying goes, 'From evildoers come
evil deeds,' so my hand will not touch you."*

1 SAMUEL 24:12–13 NIV

David, who spoke the words in today's verses, was one of the kings of Israel. Saul, the king who ruled before David, hated David and continually tried to kill him. David finally had the opportunity to kill Saul, but instead he let him go free. (An action that completely confused David's men!)

David realized if he took matters into his own hands, he'd be just like his enemies. Instead, he handed vengeance over to the Lord, trusting God would take care of justice.

The opportunity to get revenge on someone almost always looks satisfying. By retaliating, you're putting yourself on their level. Instead, hand vengeance over to God. The peace knowing you did what's right is a much better reward.

. . . .

*Father God, help me put my
desire for vengeance into Your hands.*

Share Your Wisdom

*The heartfelt counsel of a friend is
as sweet as perfume and incense.*
PROVERBS 27:9 NLT

Your sense of smell is closely linked to your feelings. Walking into your house and smelling freshly baked cookies makes you feel excited, loved, and secure. Waking up to the smell of smoke, however, would bring panic and confusion because, based on that smell, you know something's wrong.

One of the kindest things you can do for a friend is listen to their hurts and offer them counsel. Your wisdom and encouragement can bring them a huge amount of comfort and peace. Genuine, heartfelt advice from a friend brings the comfort, warmth, and peace of a sweet, enjoyable smell.

. . . .

*Dear Jesus, help my advice be heartfelt
and pure. Give me wisdom to encourage
my friends when they need it.*

Sympathetic Friendship

Now when Job's three friends heard of all this adversity that had come upon him, they came each one from his own place, Eliphaz the Temanite, Bildad the Shuhite and Zophar the Naamathite; and they made an appointment together to come to sympathize with him and comfort him.

JOB 2:11 NASB

When disaster struck Job, his friends initially did the right thing: they showed up to sympathize and comfort him. As time passed though, they began lecturing Job, assuming his sins were causing his misfortunes. They went from friends to critics because they didn't understand the whole situation.

When tragedy strikes, or keeps striking, it's easy to wonder, *What did they do to deserve this?* It's not our place to judge why someone is put through certain hardships. Instead, we must continue being sympathetic to those going through difficult times, no matter how long the season lasts.

. . . .

Make me a sympathetic and comforting friend, Jesus. Help me love my friends without judging their situation.

Determine to Go

And Elijah said to Elisha, "Please stay here, for the
Lord has sent me as far as Bethel." But Elisha said,
"As the Lord lives, and as you yourself live, I will
not leave you." So they went down to Bethel.
2 Kings 2:2 esv

Elijah and Elisha had a unique bond, and not just because their names were similar. They were both prophets of God, tasked with telling the Israelites what God wanted of them.

Elijah mentored Elisha, and as he completed his final days of ministry before being brought to heaven, he let Elisha off the hook and told him to stay while he traveled to finish the work God gave him. Elisha didn't quit though. He determined to go with Elijah and continue learning from him until the very end.

As you pursue kindness, closely follow those living obedient, kind lives. Shadow them and spend time with them, learning from their wisdom and ministry so that you can also live a life pleasing to the Lord.

Dear Lord, please bring me good mentors
and make me a devoted mentee!

Faithful with Little

"After a long time their master returned from his trip and called them to give an account of how they had used his money. The servant to whom he had entrusted the five bags of silver came forward with five more and said, 'Master, you gave me five bags of silver to invest, and I have earned five more.' The master was full of praise. 'Well done, my good and faithful servant. You have been faithful in handling this small amount, so now I will give you many more responsibilities. Let's celebrate together!'"
MATTHEW 25:19–21 NLT

You don't have to become a famous singer, champion athlete, or renowned scientist to make God proud of you. All you have to do is take what He's given you and use it for His glory. Whatever talent God's bestowed on you, be it grand or humble, take it and use it for His kingdom.

. . . .

Dear Lord, help me use my talents for Your glory.

Be Still

"Be still, and know that I am God. I will be exalted among the nations, I will be exalted in the earth!"
PSALM 46:10 ESV

Most of us don't know how to be still. Even when our bodies aren't moving, our minds go a million miles a minute. We wonder how on earth we're going to get all our homework done or whether we'll make varsity volleyball. We wonder if anyone's Snapped us or how our newest Instagram selfie is doing. We escape to the world of Fortnite or fantasize about getting invited into the popular group at school.

As you go about your day, practice taking "stillness breaks" and pray this prayer: "Lord, You are God. Be exalted in my life." Learning to be still keeps your focus on the beauty, kindness, and goodness of God and not the distractions of the world.

Dear God, I need Your help being still.
Gently remind me to quiet my mind
and focus on the fact that YOU are God.

Beautiful Reconciliation

*Then Esau ran to meet him and embraced
him, threw his arms around his neck,
and kissed him. And they both wept.*
GENESIS 33:4 NLT

Have you ever expected something to go terribly, but it ended up going well?

Esau and his twin brother, Jacob, had been fighting many years. At the height of their feud, Jacob tricked Esau out of his inheritance and Esau threatened to kill Jacob. Jacob fled, and they didn't see each other for a long time.

Years later, Jacob realized he was about to cross paths with his estranged brother. Desiring reconciliation, Jacob sent peace offerings to Esau, but cell phones didn't exist yet, so he had no way of knowing if these gifts did anything to appease his brother's anger. Instead of seeking revenge, Esau surprised Jacob by greeting him with love and kindness. Esau had let go of his hatred, and the reconciliation was beautiful and unexpected, a picture of what can happen when we stop letting hatred control our lives.

· ·

*Father God, help me forgive and reconcile
where I've been holding on to hatred.*

Washing Feet

*Then he poured water into a basin and began
to wash the disciples' feet and to wipe them
with the towel that was wrapped around him.*
JOHN 13:5 ESV

During biblical times, many people wore sandals or
went barefoot, so before entering a home it was cus-
tomary to wash your feet (similar to how we take off our
shoes before entering a house). Often a slave or servant
did the actual foot washing of houseguests. It was considered the lowliest job, and for good reason. Foot wash-
ers physically lowered themselves in order to scrub the
dirt and muck from someone else's feet.

Jesus lowered Himself to the humblest position in
humanity in order to wash us clean. Washing His disciples' feet pointed to a bigger, more important cleansing:
the cleansing of our sins on the cross.

* *

*Dear Jesus, You gave us such a powerful
example of humbly serving others. Make
me willing to lower myself to serve others.*

A Beautiful Neighborhood

*"Also, seek the peace and prosperity of the city to which
I have carried you into exile. Pray to the LORD for it,
because if it prospers, you too will prosper."*
JEREMIAH 29:7 NIV

The Israelites had been forced out of their homeland
and into a foreign city. The Lord told them not to isolate
and withdraw but to live fully and seek the welfare of
their new community.

We're currently exiles on earth, waiting for our
permanent home in heaven. Rather than avoid getting
involved in our communities, we should do whatever
we can to make the place where we live prosper. Think
about ways you can make a difference in your neighbor-
hood. Building up your community shows the people
you live around that Jesus cares for them.

*Dear Lord, I want to help make the place where
I live peaceful and prosperous. Put on my heart
ways that I can serve and build up my community.*

Eternity and Beyond

When all the people of Israel saw the fire coming down and the glorious presence of the LORD filling the Temple, they fell face down on the ground and worshiped and praised the LORD, saying, "He is good! His faithful love endures forever!"

2 CHRONICLES 7:3 NLT

Imagine seeing God's glory displayed in a powerful and miraculous way. This is what the Israelites had just witnessed, and the experience drove them to their knees. They praised the Lord and His everlasting love.

Because we live within time, it's hard for us to completely understand the concept of "forever." We only know what it means to have a beginning, middle, and end.

One day our eyes will be opened, and we'll fully grasp eternity and God's unending love. Our Father's love never lessens, runs out, or gets bored. Our loving God remains faithful to His people to eternity and beyond.

Wow, I can't fathom what eternity looks like.
Thank You, God, for Your faithful love
and that it lasts forever and ever.

He Is God

Be not rash with your mouth, nor let your heart be hasty to utter a word before God, for God is in heaven and you are on earth. Therefore let your words be few.
ECCLESIASTES 5:2 ESV

Have you ever been angry at God? He's all-powerful and He could give us what we want, so when He doesn't, it's easy to get mad and turn away from Him.

Be quick to remember that God is on the throne above. He knows all, sees all, and still deeply cares for you and your desires.

Approach the throne of God with praise and humility, even when He's keeping you from what you want. He loves you more than you know, and though you wear blinders now, one day you'll see that every no was really a yes to your greater good.

- -

I'm sorry for the times I've gotten angry at You, God. I don't always understand why You say no, especially to things that seem good. Help me trust Your answer and praise You anyway.

Assume the Best

*Make every effort to keep the unity of
the Spirit through the bond of peace.*
EPHESIANS 4:3 NIV

*Macie never responded to my Snap. I know she's looked
at her phone,* Lauren thought. *I bet she's just being rude.*

The next day at school, Lauren went out of her way
to ignore Macie. Then she overheard Macie telling
someone that she'd dropped her phone and was waiting
on a new one.

Oops, thought Lauren. *I guess she wasn't being rude.*

It's easy to jump to conclusions about someone's
behavior. They pass us in the hallway without a hello,
don't respond to a text, or say something confusing and
we assume they're mad, rude, or insensitive. If you don't
know the whole situation, try not to judge a person's
motives. Assuming the best about someone is a way of
being kind.

. . . .

*Dear Lord, I want to be gracious toward
others. Help me give the benefit of the
doubt when a situation isn't clear.*

Flexible Plans

Come now, you who say, "Today or tomorrow we will go into such and such a town and spend a year there and trade and make a profit"—yet you do not know what tomorrow will bring. What is your life? For you are a mist that appears for a little time and then vanishes.
JAMES 4:13–14 ESV

Planning is a way of stewarding the time God's given you. However, many opportunities for kindness require flexibility and a willingness to lay aside your plans in order to be present and helpful to someone in need.

Just as steam disappears moments after swirling up from a boiling pot, our lives go by incredibly quickly (even though they seem long!). Opportunities for kindness may not happen tomorrow, so when a chance to do good arises, bring it before the Lord in that moment and determine if He wants you to exchange your premade plans for His last-minute ones.

· ·

Dear Jesus, please make me someone who holds plans loosely, always willing to lay down my own will for what You want me to do.

Practice Immediately

But prove yourselves doers of the word,
and not merely hearers who delude themselves.
JAMES 1:22 NASB

I used to teach piano lessons, and over the years I noticed two different kinds of students. The first kind of student went home and practiced what they learned immediately after the lesson. They always remembered what they'd been taught and advanced quickly. The second kind of student put off practicing and almost always forgot what they'd been taught. They had to relearn everything each week and progressed slowly.

When God teaches you something, put it into practice right away. If today you read about being slow to speak, in your next conversation, try to listen more than you talk. If you hear a lesson about humility, don't go around bragging about your accomplishments.

By practicing what you've learned, the Word of God will take root in your life and you'll begin growing. Don't say, "That's okay, I'll start tomorrow," for tomorrow never actually arrives.

. . . .

I want to be someone who doesn't just hear Your Word,
Lord, but does it. Send Your Holy Spirit to guide me
and to remind me to practice what You've taught me.

Know Why

We, though, are going to love—love and be loved.
First we were loved, now we love. He loved us first.
1 JOHN 4:19 MSG

If we're going to be ambassadors of kindness to our family, friends, and community, we must know *why* we're supposed to show love.

We show love because God loved us *first*. We extend love and kindness to others because God extended them to us when we were still dead in our sins. He set the example for kindness, forgiveness, and sacrifice when He sent Jesus to live the life we should've lived, die the death we deserved, and conquer death through the resurrection.

Dear God, thank You for modeling perfect
love for us. I pray that I can extend the love
You've shown me to others and that through
my kindness people will come to know You.

Works on Parade

*"But when you give to the poor, do not let your left
hand know what your right hand is doing, so that
your giving will be in secret; and your Father who
sees what is done in secret will reward you."*
MATTHEW 6:3–4 NASB

When Nadia went with her church to feed the homeless downtown, she was overwhelmed by how amazing the experience made her feel. She took a few selfies with some of the kids she played with at the shelter and added them to her Instagram story. Before long, her followers began responding, telling her how amazing she was for doing such a good thing.

It's easy to casually post our good works for the world to see. Instead of posting everything, occasionally put away your phone and practice doing good things quietly and secretly. The reward God has for you in heaven will far surpass the feeling you get when the "hearts" and comments roll in.

. . . .

*Dear heavenly Father, help me to serve humbly
and to get my validation from You and not
from the response I get on social media.*

Least of These

"And he will answer, 'I tell you the truth, when you refused to help the least of these my brothers and sisters, you were refusing to help me.'"
<small>MATTHEW 25:45 NLT</small>

When you gave your life to Jesus, you became His hands and feet here on earth. If you refuse to help those around you, you're ultimately refusing to help Jesus.

Someone's status should never prevent you from helping them. Jesus, even though He was God, lowered Himself to a servant's status. He came for the "least" in the world. He came to save hurting, lost, and unseen people. By seeing those who need to be seen, hearing those who need to be heard, and helping those who need to be helped, you continue Jesus' mission to bring hope to *all* people.

. . . .

Dear Lord, I know that I serve You by serving others. Open my eyes to the people around me who need help, and give me wisdom to know how to help them.

Foolish Wisdom

For the wisdom of this world is foolishness
in God's sight. As it is written: "He
catches the wise in their craftiness."
1 CORINTHIANS 3:19 NIV

The wisdom of this world tells you to seek security, wealth, and happiness at all costs. God tells you that in order to gain your life, you must be willing to lose it.

The wisdom of this world says, "Follow your heart!" God says, "Follow Me."

The wisdom of this world calls Godly obedience "old-fashioned" and says it stands in the way of happiness. God calls the obedient and pure in heart "blessed."

. . . .

I want to live according to Your wisdom,
God, and not the world's wisdom. Help me
put aside what the world says and follow You.

Learning to Comfort Others

All praise to the God and Father of our Master,
Jesus the Messiah! Father of all mercy! God of
all healing counsel! He comes alongside us when
we go through hard times, and before you know it,
he brings us alongside someone else who is going
through hard times so that we can be there for
that person just as God was there for us.
2 CORINTHIANS 1:3–4 MSG

When you're hurting, the Lord comes by your side and comforts you. In comforting you, He's also showing you how to help others during their difficult times. Let's take a moment and become students of how God comforts His children.

The Lord comforts by bringing peace—He reassures us that our trials won't last forever. The Lord comforts gently—He understands that our pain is real and deep. The Lord comforts patiently—He knows that the path to recovery takes time. And the Lord comforts by staying at our side the entire journey.

Now let's go comfort others with peace, gentleness, patience, and love, just as God has comforted us.

* *

Dear God, make me someone who comforts
others like You have comforted me.

Courageous Kindness

*"This is my command—be strong and courageous!
Do not be afraid or discouraged. For the LORD
your God is with you wherever you go."*
JOSHUA 1:9 NLT

As Avery sat at her usual lunch table, she noticed a new girl sitting by herself. She felt a tug on her heart to go and talk to her, but she suddenly became afraid.

Maybe she wants *to be alone,* Avery thought. *I don't want to bother her.*

Sometimes an act of kindness requires vulnerability and bravery. When we answer God's call to kindness, we risk rejection, ridicule, and hurt.

Remember, God stays with you wherever you go. He's actively guiding you and emboldening you through the Holy Spirit. Your job is to obey what God's asked you to do. Don't get discouraged if the results aren't exactly what you wanted. Whether or not circumstances go your way, your obedience pleases your Father in heaven.

* * *

*Thank You for always being with me, Lord
God! Make me bold and courageous
with my kindness, starting today!*

Growing Up

Rather, speaking the truth in love, we are to grow up
in every way into him who is the head, into Christ.
EPHESIANS 4:15 ESV

One of my favorite movies to watch as a child was *Peter
Pan*, the story about a boy who avoids growing up by
living in a place called Neverland. I loved the idea of
staying a kid forever.

Maybe you're eager to grow up, or maybe you want
to stay young and carefree. No matter your thoughts on
getting older, God doesn't want you to stay the same.
You're supposed to mature, transform, and "grow up"
spiritually. As you walk in the footsteps of Jesus toward
spiritual maturity, you'll learn to deliver truth in love,
respond with grace, and forgive readily.

. . . .

Dear Jesus, I want to follow in Your footsteps
and become a spiritual adult. Help me
grow in grace, love, and forgiveness.

Our Firm Foundation

Rejoice in our confident hope.
Be patient in trouble, and keep on praying.
ROMANS 12:12 NLT

Life, as you probably already know, doesn't always go your way.

If you put your hope in your circumstances, you'll be disappointed often. If your hope is in what Jesus accomplished on the cross, then your foundation is firm. The ups and downs of life may shake you, but you won't be destroyed.

One day, Jesus will return and suffering will be no more—so continue doing good, being kind, and showing love. Be patient when life gets difficult, and no matter what happens, don't stop praying. Our prayers are special to God. They're woven into the story as God works behind the scenes to bring lost souls to Himself.

· ·

Father God, I know it's important to have a firm
foundation—one that won't be destroyed when life
gets hard. Keep me rooted to the truth, and make
me patient through life's ups and downs.

The Lord Is for You

The LORD is for me; I will not fear;
what can man do to me?
PSALM 118:6 NASB

What can man do to me?! you might be thinking after reading this verse. *People can do a lot of damage! They can insult me, reject me, and hurt me!*

Now ask yourself this question: "What can people do to me that would destroy my salvation and eternity with Jesus in heaven?"

The answer is "Nothing!"

People can hurt us, insult us, and let us down in many ways. But if Jesus is your Savior, there's good news: no one can do anything to end that relationship. When the Lord is on your side, your eternal security is safe from the world.

. . . .

I don't want to live my life in fear, Lord God,
but people do some pretty wicked things. Give me
peace when people are cruel. Remind me of Your
promise that nothing can separate me from Your love.

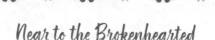

Near to the Brokenhearted

*The LORD is near to the brokenhearted
and saves the crushed in spirit.*
PSALM 34:18 ESV

If you've experienced crushing loss or had your heart broken so deeply that breathing hurts, then Jesus has made Himself known to you in a unique way. You've seen a side of God that's impossible to experience when life is going well.

Jesus knows your pain because He experienced suffering while on earth. He doesn't abandon you in your time of need. He draws near, lifting your burdens and gently reminding you of His love.

· ·

Dear Lord, draw near to me when life feels crushing.

The Weeds of Bitterness

*See to it that no one falls short of the grace
of God and that no bitter root grows up
to cause trouble and defile many.*
HEBREWS 12:15 NIV

In food, a bitter taste is characterized by a sharp lack of sweetness. Bitter ingredients must be added carefully to recipes because they can quickly overpower all other flavors.

Even a little bit of bitterness can destroy your ability to see the blessings God's given you. When you let resentment into your life, you'll feel cheated by everything, and before you know it, your bitterness will begin spreading to those around you.

Kindness can't blossom in a heart overrun with the weeds of bitterness. When you notice a root of bitterness springing up, pull it out immediately. Take it to God and let Him destroy it. By destroying bitterness, you'll create room for the seeds of kindness to sprout and grow.

. . . .

*Dear Jesus, sometimes life seems unfair.
Teach me to focus on my blessings, and replace
all my bitter roots with seeds of kindness.*

Foundation of Confidence

*But now thus says the LORD, he who created
you, O Jacob, he who formed you, O Israel:
"Fear not, for I have redeemed you; I have
called you by name, you are mine."*
ISAIAH 43:1 ESV

Do you have a favorite celebrity? Think about how important you'd feel if a famous person not only *knew* your name but posted to the entire world on Instagram that you were their friend. Can you imagine the confidence you'd have knowing they had your back?

God not only calls you by name, but He's announced to the world that you belong to Him. Hold your head up high, because you're personally known by the most important being in the universe—the Creator! He formed you, redeemed you, and claims you as His own. Let that truth provide the foundation for your confidence.

. . . .

*Thank You for calling me by name, Lord!
Let my confidence be secure, knowing
that I am loved and chosen by You.*

Consecrated Days

"Before I formed you in the womb I knew you,
and before you were born I consecrated you;
I have appointed you a prophet to the nations."
JEREMIAH 1:5 NASB

Jeremiah was a prophet in the Old Testament tasked by God to speak truth—sometimes very difficult truth—to the Israelites. God told Jeremiah He created him and specifically formed him for this calling.

If you're a child of God, then He's planned your days and prepared you for what He's called you to do. He shaped you uniquely, knowing when and where you'd be alive. Your personality, talents, and skills are no accident—God gave them to you to impact your school, home, and community for His kingdom.

• •

Dear Lord, I know You've prepared me for what You've
called me to do. When life surprises me, I need to
remember that nothing catches You off guard.

God's Voice

"When he has brought out all his own,
he goes before them, and the sheep
follow him, for they know his voice."
JOHN 10:4 ESV

If you go to the country of Ireland, you'll often find lots of sheep from different farms pasturing on the same hillside. When it's time to separate them and bring them back, shepherds know their sheep by their markings, and the sheep know their shepherd's voice. If a sheep doesn't recognize its shepherd's voice, it will end up alone or with the wrong flock.

We must learn to hear God's voice amid the noise of this world. We learn to hear God's voice by studying the Bible, praying, and meditating. If we don't connect to our Shepherd daily, all the distractions in our lives will drown out His voice, and we'll miss opportunities for kindness because we didn't hear Him calling us.

. . . .

Teach me to recognize Your voice, Lord God.
I want to follow where You lead.

Hunting for Kindness

*Whoever goes hunting for what is right
and kind finds life itself—glorious life!*
PROVERBS 21:21 MSG

If you're like me, you probably haven't had to hunt for your food. (Unless you count finding what you need in a grocery store as hunting.) Hunting requires work, skill, and practice. You could sit around and wait for an animal to come to you, but you'll have more opportunities for food if you get up and *go* to places inhabited by animals.

Instead of waiting for things to fall into your lap, actively hunt for opportunities to do good. Be on the lookout for needs that you can fill.

Proactive hunters are rewarded with food. If we proactively seek out opportunities for kindness, we'll find something even greater—life! Not just *any* life, but *glorious* life! Doing what's right brings the best reward: favor with the One who created you.

. . . .

*Dear God, I'm going to actively look for places
where Your love is needed. Give me the strength
and wisdom to be a kindness hunter.*

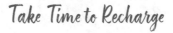

Take Time to Recharge

*After sending them home, he went
up into the hills by himself to pray.
Night fell while he was there alone.*
MATTHEW 14:23 NLT

No one understands the demands of the world better than Jesus. As word got out about His ministry, more and more people came to be healed and taught by Him. Jesus retreated often to connect with God and recharge. He knew He wouldn't be able to complete His mission if He didn't spend time alone with His Father.

It's important to carve out time to recharge and connect to God. Be intentional about this time. It may mean turning off your phone, skipping out on a trip to the movies with your friends, or going for a walk or somewhere quiet. By taking time to renew your energy and restore your spirit, you'll be better prepared to live a life of love and kindness.

* *

*Dear Lord, give me opportunities to recharge
so that I can continue living on mission for You.*

Living as a Cultivator

*Then the LORD God took the man and put him
into the garden of Eden to cultivate it and keep it.*
GENESIS 2:15 NASB

Even before humans fell into rebellion, God gave them work. At the beginning of creation, God put Adam and Eve into the garden and told them to cultivate what He'd created.

There are many different ways to develop and cultivate the world God created. We cultivate culture through music, dance, and art. We cultivate order through work, routine, government, and responsibly taking care of our environment. Finally, we cultivate relationships through kindness, gentleness, and love.

. . . .

*I know it's important to be a good steward of
what You've created, Father God. I'm going
to try my best to look for ways to encourage,
support, and cultivate what You've created.*

What Is God Doing?

*If people can't see what God is doing, they stumble
all over themselves; but when they attend to
what he reveals, they are most blessed.*
PROVERBS 29:18 MSG

Almost every activity comes with a certain goal. Cooks
work to make delicious meals. Athletes train in hopes of
one day winning a medal. Writers carefully craft words,
eagerly anticipating the release of their finished book.

Without a vision or goal, our work lacks direction
and motivation. Fortunately, God's shared His vision
with us: bring light to the darkness and point lost souls
toward Christ. Everything we do, if done for God, plays
a role in that vision.

When you show kindness, you're not just being nice
for the sake of it; you're actively participating in God's
vision to bring love to a hurting world.

* * *

*Dear God, keep Your vision alive in me.
Holy Spirit, remind me often of the
bigger picture that I'm part of.*

Living Sacrifice

*Therefore, I urge you, brothers and sisters,
in view of God's mercy, to offer your bodies as
a living sacrifice, holy and pleasing to God—
this is your true and proper worship.*

ROMANS 12:1 NIV

Sometimes we think of "worship" as the singing part of a church service, but any activity done to bring glory and honor to God is an act of worship.

This means we can worship God all day, every day, simply by living in a way that honors Him. We express love, devotion, and adoration to God when we obey what He's called us to do.

For example, your act of kindness brings adoration to the name of God. Your decision to love difficult people expresses your devotion to God. Getting some friends together for a game night blesses the heart of God because He loves to see His children getting along and enjoying His gifts.

*Dear heavenly Father, You're worthy of continuous
praise, honor, and glory. I want to worship
You constantly in the way I live my life.*

Eagerly Receive the Word

Now these were more noble-minded than those in Thessalonica, for they received the word with great eagerness, examining the Scriptures daily to see whether these things were so.

ACTS 17:11 NASB

Do you do devotions out of obligation? As part of a checklist? Or do you eagerly search the Word of God to learn more about Jesus and how you can live for Him?

Studying scripture can sometimes feel like a chore. At first glance much of the Bible appears boring and irrelevant. However, the more we study God's Word, the more we see that it's still living, active, and applicable to our lives today!

When we read and study scriptures (even the "boring" parts), we learn more about God and what He desires of us. As we learn more about the heart of God, we become more eager to please Him with our attitude and actions.

. . . .

Thank You, Father God, for revealing Yourself in the scriptures. I don't ever want to take Your Word for granted. Make me someone who's eager to study the Bible and learn more about You.

Springs of Life

Keep your heart with all vigilance,
for from it flow the springs of life.
PROVERBS 4:23 ESV

Many rivers originate from springs. The springs overflow from the ground and turn into a river. The purer the springs, the purer the water that comes from them.

Your heart harbors the springs of life. What grows in your heart will eventually spill over into your behavior, no matter how well you think you can hide it.

All actions, whether good or bad, begin in the heart. A heart filled with bitterness will spring into a life of anger and spitefulness. But a heart filled with the love of God will spring into a life of kindness.

. . . .

Dear Jesus, I want my heart to be a
spring of love and kindness. Help me
stay vigilant and keep my heart pure.

More Blessed to Give

"And I have been a constant example of how
you can help those in need by working hard.
You should remember the words of the Lord Jesus:
'It is more blessed to give than to receive.'"
ACTS 20:35 NLT

Gifts, especially thoughtful ones, make you feel loved, valued, and important. It's always a blessing to receive something you want or need. You'll receive an even bigger blessing, however, when you're the one doing the giving. Giving brings inexplicable joy and purpose to the giver.

Money and presents aren't the only ways to give. You can bless others by giving them your time, your energy, or some encouraging words.

No matter what you give, you can never out-give what God's given you: grace through Jesus Christ.

• •

Dear Jesus, please bless me as I look
for ways to give to those around me!

The Good of Others

No one should seek their own good,
but the good of others.
1 CORINTHIANS 10:24 NIV

When I was growing up, my mom had a strange rule in our house during birthday parties: the birthday girl or boy got served last. The guests were to receive food, cake, and drinks *before* the person being celebrated.

I didn't understand it at the time, but this rule taught me and my siblings how to love like Christ. Even though we were the ones being celebrated, we had the responsibility of making sure everyone else was taken care of first. Jesus, who deserves to be the most celebrated One in the universe, put everyone else's needs ahead of His own when He came to earth.

. . . .

Father God, it's so easy to get caught up in
what I want and need. Make me someone
who thinks about the needs of those around
me more than I think about my own needs.

Do the Right Thing

*So whoever knows the right thing to
do and fails to do it, for him it is sin.*
JAMES 4:17 ESV

Alexa listened in the locker room as two of her friends talked about another girl in their grade. She knew the things they said were untrue and, in all honesty, pretty mean.

If I say something, they'll just turn on me, she thought. *As long as I'm not talking about her too, I'm not doing anything wrong.*

We often think of sin as something we *do*. However, sin can easily be something we *don't* do. If we see an opportunity to do what we know is right and pass it up because we don't want to be inconvenienced or are afraid it'll turn out bad for us, then we're also sinning.

• •

Dear God, forgive me for the times I've looked the other way when I should've done or said something. Give me the strength and wisdom to do what I know is right.

Pursue Peace

If it is possible, as far as it depends
on you, live at peace with everyone.
ROMANS 12:18 NIV

Always choose the path that leads to peace. If it's within your power to forgive, apologize, or respond gently, then choose that response. Become someone who seeks harmony as the final destination.

Unfortunately, even if you do the right thing, you won't always be able to live at peace with everyone. Some people love drama and continuously provoke, gossip, and hold grudges no matter what you do to keep the peace. Don't let this kind of person draw you into their world. Keep "high-drama" people at a distance, and continue to be a peacekeeper, not a troublemaker.

* *

Dear heavenly Father, I know it's important
to live at peace with those around me.
Make me the kind of person who takes the
first step to reconcile with someone.

All Things Made New

And He who sits on the throne said, "Behold,
I am making all things new." And He said,
"Write, for these words are faithful and true."
REVELATION 21:5 NASB

Choosing kindness isn't always easy, especially when you get tired, annoyed, and run down. Kindness sometimes feels like trudging up a big hill on a hot day.

Someday Jesus will return, and God will make the heavens and earth new. Those who trusted Jesus for their salvation will live in a world of beautiful, uninterrupted peace.

Once we're in eternity, choosing kindness won't take any effort. It'll be as easy as breathing. We won't have to fight our urge to disobey or act selfishly. We'll be able to relax and enjoy eternity in the presence of God.

* *

I can't wait for heaven, God. Thank You
for giving me the hope of eternity with You.
Remind me of this promise during hard days.

A Kindness Loan

Whoever is kind to the poor lends to the LORD,
and he will reward them for what they have done.
PROVERBS 19:17 NIV

Caring for the poor touches the heart of God. Serving others brings you closer to God, who sees and cares for all people without any favoritism.

What's more, the Lord promises to fill those who pour into others. He repays those who extend kindness to people in need. The Lord doesn't ever waste a loan of kindness. He rewards it with joy, peace, and a deposit in your heavenly bank account.

* *

Dear Lord, break my heart for what breaks
Yours. Bring me ideas on how to serve
the poor in my community.

Shine a Light

"In the same way, let your light shine before others, so that they may see your good works and give glory to your Father who is in heaven."
MATTHEW 5:16 ESV

Earlier in this book we talked about a verse in Matthew warning us against parading our good works in front of others (Matthew 6:3). So how do we shine our light if we're supposed to keep good deeds a secret?

We're not supposed to brag, purposefully draw attention to ourselves, or fish for compliments about our works. But people will see our kindness the same way they see a light shining on a hill during a dark night. In this selfish world, selflessness burns bright.

Also, we're never supposed to hide the *reason* for our kindness. If people notice your good works, share with them about the even greater love and kindness of our God.

. . . .

Dear Lord, let my kindness and my actions shine a light that leads people to You.

Love Covers Conflict

Hatred stirs up conflict,
but love covers over all wrongs.
PROVERBS 10:12 NIV

When you hold on to hatred, you leave doors wide open for conflict to enter your life. You'll become consumed with getting back at people who've wronged you. Giving your heart over to hate allows your own wound to fester and grow.

There's a better option available for handling those who've hurt you: love. Love cools hatred like aloe cools a bad sunburn.

Love might mean forgiving someone but keeping your distance if they're continuously mean. Love might mean having a conversation with a friend who wronged you so you can make amends. Or love might mean accepting an apology and not bringing up the offense again.

I want to choose love over hatred, Lord, but sometimes I don't know how! Change my heart, and show me how to be kind to people who make it difficult to love.

No Divisions

*There is neither Jew nor Gentile, neither slave
nor free, nor is there male and female,
for you are all one in Christ Jesus.*
<small>GALATIANS 3:28 NIV</small>

A Sunday school teacher I had as a kid used to say, "The ground is level at the foot of the cross."

Humans like to categorize each other based on background, race, education, wealth, looks, gender, or anything else that sets them apart. But God doesn't divide people this way. He shows no preference or special treatment for any particular group. Everyone is equal in the eyes of the Savior, and we're all sinners in need of Jesus' saving grace.

We must see people, no matter how different they are from us, as God sees them: beautiful, unique, and worthy of love. God created humanity to be very diverse, and He considers every single one of His children His favorite.

• •

*You love all people equally, God. Help me treat
everyone as Jesus would treat them and not
see differences as a negative thing.*

People Over Things

"Give to anyone who asks; and when things are taken away from you, don't try to get them back."
LUKE 6:30 NLT

One time I loaned a set of DVDs (this was in the dark ages before everything was streaming) to a friend. This particular series held a special place in my heart, and I wanted my set back when she was finished. Long story short, she never returned them and said that she didn't remember borrowing them. I was hurt and a little mad that she had treated my things so carelessly.

The Lord gently spoke to my heart and reminded me that my DVDs were replaceable. My friendship with this person was not. I could stay mad and risk destroying the friendship, or I could believe her when she said she didn't remember taking them.

Jesus calls us to do some pretty radical things, like not getting attached to material things and forgiving quickly when we don't get our possessions back.

. . . .

Dear Jesus, it's very hard when people take advantage of my generosity. Help me give freely and not get attached to material things.

Do Your Possessions Own You?

*Some people are always greedy
for more, but the godly love to give!*
PROVERBS 21:26 NLT

Some people never seem to be happy with what they have. The excitement of new stuff wears off quickly, and they need something even brighter, trendier, and faster to hold their attention.

If what you already have doesn't satisfy you, getting even more of it won't change anything. You can have the newest phone, wear the latest fashions, and play the latest games, but none of those things will leave you feeling fulfilled in the long run.

People who aren't owned by their things love to give. Generous people find joy, hope, and fulfillment in living openhandedly.

* *

*Dear Jesus, You gave everything for me
on the cross. I want to be someone who
loves to give and lives with open hands.*

Different Gifts

*We have different gifts, according to the grace
given to each of us. If your gift is prophesying,
then prophesy in accordance with your faith; if it is
serving, then serve; if it is teaching, then teach;
if it is to encourage, then give encouragement; if it
is giving, then give generously; if it is to lead, do it
diligently; if it is to show mercy, do it cheerfully.*
ROMANS 12:6–8 NIV

Don't compare your gifts to other people's. No two people have been given the exact same calling, which means no two people will have the exact same set of gifts and talents. God has equipped *you* for the path *you're* on.

So celebrate the abilities of others, but also appreciate your own gifts. Don't waste lots of time and energy wishing you had what someone else has. Instead, spend that time doing what God's created you to do. Whatever your gift, live it out with excellence and joy.

*Thank You, Lord, for the gifts You've given
me and the calling You've placed on my life.*

Don't Mock the Hurting

Whoever mocks the poor insults his Maker;
he who is glad at calamity will not go unpunished.
PROVERBS 17:5 ESV

Have you ever, even for a split second, been happy when something bad happens to someone? Maybe they're not the nicest person and you feel like they finally got what they deserved. Or maybe watching someone else fail made you feel better about your failures.

Making fun of someone who's poor or rejoicing over someone's failure insults our Creator. We should always try to help and build up those who are down. Don't mock, tease, or assume they somehow deserve what they got. Understanding and kindness go a long way when someone's experiencing hurt and rejection.

. . . .

Dear God, turn me into someone who always comforts
and helps others. I don't want to be someone who
ridicules and mocks people when they're down.

Filled by God

Then God said, "I give you every seed-bearing plant on the face of the whole earth and every tree that has fruit with seed in it. They will be yours for food. And to all the beasts of the earth and all the birds in the sky and all the creatures that move along the ground— everything that has the breath of life in it—I give every green plant for food." And it was so.

GENESIS 1:29–30 NIV

God created all things to be filled. He created the earth to be filled with oceans and mountains and multitudes of living things. He created humans to be filled with His living Spirit. When we allow the Lord's Spirit to fill us, then kindness and goodness become a natural part of our lives. When kindness and goodness become a natural part of our lives, we'll begin to see our homes, schools, and communities transformed by the love of God.

. . . .

Dear Lord, fill me with Your Holy Spirit! Let my life be overflowing with love and kindness.

Keep Praying

*So we have not stopped praying for you since
we first heard about you. We ask God to give
you complete knowledge of his will and to give
you spiritual wisdom and understanding.*
COLOSSIANS 1:9 NLT

The best gifts God can give us are wisdom and understanding. God tells us that anyone who asks for wisdom will be given it generously (James 1:5).

We often pray and ask God to change or fix a certain situation and then wonder why He's not answering our prayer. Wisdom and understanding allow us a little glimpse behind the scenes of what God's doing.

Continue praying, asking for all things, but especially that God might give you and other believers insight into His good and perfect will.

* *

*Father God, please give me and other
believers spiritual wisdom and understanding.
Give us eyes to see what You're doing.*

God's Loving Protection

Praise the LORD, for he has shown me the
wonders of his unfailing love. He kept me
safe when my city was under attack.
PSALM 31:21 NLT

What plagues your thoughts, dear one? What keeps you up at night and robs you of peace? What continuously attacks your joy?

The Lord's love never fails. He never takes a day off from watching over His children. He protects you from the evil of the world and is on hand to fight your battles.

We don't know what tomorrow may bring, but God's grace is already in the future, working everything together for our good.

. . . .

Dear Jesus, I ask that You protect
me from harm and give me peace.

Tell the World!

*I will tell of the LORD's unfailing love. I will
praise the LORD for all he has done. I will rejoice
in his great goodness to Israel, which he has
granted according to his mercy and love.*

ISAIAH 63:7 NLT

When something incredible happens, people eagerly catch it on their phones and share it with the world. Really remarkable stories continue getting shared and go viral.

It's hard to keep amazing things to yourself. You want to shout to the world about the goal you accomplished, the goodness you witnessed, or the victory you experienced.

When wonderful things happen, take time to praise God for His faithfulness and thank Him for His favor toward you. When God does something incredible, share it with others so that they too can know the wondrous love of our Lord!

* * *

*Lord, You're magnificent, mighty, and Your
love for me is never ending. Thank You for
Your blessings and great faithfulness! I'm not
going to keep secret all You've done for me!*

Better Than Life

*Because Your lovingkindness is better
than life, my lips will praise You.*
PSALM 63:3 NASB

Think of the best day you've ever had. Now think about what made that day so incredible. Was it the quality time with family and friends? An exciting new adventure? Or was it just a twenty-four-hour period where nothing went wrong?

Now imagine an entire life filled with days like the one you remember so fondly. God's loving-kindness is better than an entire life filled with perfect days. Without His loving-kindness we can never truly live, even if we get everything we want out of this life.

*Thank You for freely giving me Your
loving-kindness, Father God. I praise
You for everything You've given me!*

The Long Wait

Don't overlook the obvious here, friends. With God, one day is as good as a thousand years, a thousand years as a day. God isn't late with his promise as some measure lateness. He is restraining himself on account of you, holding back the End because he doesn't want anyone lost. He's giving everyone space and time to change.

2 PETER 3:8–9 MSG

When God created the earth, He created time. It's strange to think about a world without clocks and calendars, right? Our perspective on time is limited, while God perfectly sees the past, present, and future from His heavenly throne.

God's timing is never late. What feels like weeks, months, or years to us may only be a moment to God. When God doesn't act according to our timetable, it's because He's acting according to His sovereign schedule, for the good of His kingdom and followers.

• •

Dear God, help me be patient and trust You when things don't happen according to my timetable.

Good Plans

This is GOD's Word on the subject: "As soon as Babylon's seventy years are up and not a day before, I'll show up and take care of you as I promised and bring you back home. I know what I'm doing. I have it all planned out—plans to take care of you, not abandon you, plans to give you the future you hope for."
JEREMIAH 29:10–11 MSG

In Old Testament times, God's people continued disobeying Him without any repentance. God allowed them to be captured by their enemy, the Babylonians, as punishment for their sins and to bring them back to obedience.

Even in their captivity though, God reassured His people that He was right by their side, caring for them and providing hope for a better future.

God's kindness fills our lives, even when He's disciplining us.

. . . .

Dear God, I know Your discipline is a form of kindness. Being in Your will is always what's best for me. Thank You for giving me hope, even when You're correcting me.

#Soulcare

But those who trust in the LORD will find new strength. They will soar high on wings like eagles. They will run and not grow weary. They will walk and not faint.
ISAIAH 40:31 NLT

Right now, #selfcare is trending on Instagram. Pictures of facials, feet sticking out of bubble baths, and quiet coffee breaks flood my feed as everyone tries to rejuvenate in a stressful world.

Self-care is ultimately a good thing because you can't pour out to others if you're running on empty. However, in order to find the strength to continue living in obedience, you must also practice soul care.

By making Bible reading, meditation, and prayer a regular part of your lifestyle, you'll continue walking the path of kindness without growing weary.

. . . .

Give me Your strength, God! Rejuvenate my spirit when I'm getting tired and stressed.

Love Is a Choice

Love is patient and kind. Love is not jealous or boastful or proud or rude. It does not demand its own way. It is not irritable, and it keeps no record of being wronged. It does not rejoice about injustice but rejoices whenever the truth wins out. Love never gives up, never loses faith, is always hopeful, and endures through every circumstance.

1 CORINTHIANS 13:4–7 NLT

Love is often treated like an uncontrollable emotion, like when someone says they're "in love." Love can definitely be a feeling, but like kindness, love is also a choice.

True, biblical love is a verb. It's an action that pursues peace and harmony. A loving person puts the good of another person ahead of their own desires.

• •

Dear Jesus, help me pursue the kind of love You describe in Your Word. I want to be known by my love for You and other people.

When Friends Fail Us

*At my first defense no one supported me, but all
deserted me; may it not be counted against them.*
2 TIMOTHY 4:16 NASB

Amy and Sophie had been friends since preschool.
They hung out all the time and didn't have any secrets
between them. Then in high school Sophie started
spending time with a different group of girls. She didn't
have much time for Amy and didn't make any attempts
to invite her into her new circle. Amy felt heartbroken
and betrayed, and she had a hard time moving past the
hurt she felt.

Maybe you've experienced something similar to
Amy. Unfortunately, friends will fail you. They'll say
something mean, they'll cancel on you for "better" plans
at the last minute, or they may abandon you completely
for a new set of friends.

This hurts. Deeply. There's no way around those
feelings. In your hurt though, seek peace with your
friend. Try to let go of their hurtful actions and don't
hold it against them. Perhaps this is a season for you to
make new friends and grow in a different way.

* *

*Please be near, Lord, when my friends hurt me.
Help me bless them even when they betray me.*

Building Spiritual Muscles

Whoever is slow to anger is better than the mighty,
and he who rules his spirit than he who takes a city.
PROVERBS 16:32 ESV

I'm not a very athletic person. It takes a lot of time and effort for me to achieve any sort of physical goals. I have to constantly force myself to continue working out, even when I don't feel like it.

As difficult as it can be to train your body, it's even harder to train your spirit. Your sinful nature constantly fights your desire to obey. The enemy uses all kinds of tactics to keep you sinning. He whispers things like, "No one will ever know"; "This will be the last time"; "They deserved it."

You must resist temptation—flee it if necessary—in order to stay away from sin. As you continue choosing obedience, your self-control muscles get stronger and resisting temptation gets easier.

. . . .

Dear Jesus, it's so hard to fight temptation
sometimes. Give me the spiritual muscles
I need to choose obedience.

In and Out of Season

Preach the word; be prepared in season and
out of season; correct, rebuke and encourage—
with great patience and careful instruction.
2 TIMOTHY 4:2 NIV

Someone once told me that the only thing constant in life is change, which I've found to be true. Life is full of transitions. Fall rolls into winter, people transition into new seasons, and even that one thing you counted on to stay consistent may change without warning.

Unlike life, God never changes. His Word remains constant in a world of perpetual change. No matter what's going on around you, God's call to live according to His will stands in place.

You won't be able to control much of what happens to you in this life, but you can rest knowing your job is to respond to all circumstances with kindness, joy, and love.

. . . .

Dear Jesus, make Your Word my anchor. No matter
how much changes in my life, I want to respond to it
obediently and always show kindness and love.

Repent with Your Heart

"Don't tear your clothing in your grief, but tear
your hearts instead." Return to the LORD your
God, for he is merciful and compassionate,
slow to get angry and filled with unfailing love.
He is eager to relent and not punish.
JOEL 2:13 NLT

Are you a perfectionist? Extreme perfectionists often have a hard time accepting grace and forgiveness. They feel like they need to be punished or make things right before they can move on.

God isn't interested in outward, self-inflicted punishment. God wants our hearts broken by sin, but He also wants them healed by His love. A heart that's been broken by sin and mended by grace makes a big impact for the kingdom.

When you fail, don't beat yourself up or give in to self-pity. Learn from your mistake and run toward God, knowing that He fully forgives you and embraces you in His unfailing love.

. . . .

Thank You for Your compassion and forgiveness, God.
I'm glad I can run to You when I mess up. Help me grow
from my mistakes and not let them hold me back.

God Sees Your Efforts

"I see everything you're doing for me. Impressive!
The love and the faith, the service and persistence.
Yes, very impressive! You get better at it every day.
But why do you let that Jezebel who calls herself
a prophet mislead my dear servants into Cross-
denying, self-indulging religion?"
REVELATION 2:19–20 MSG

When musicians consistently practice their instrument, they improve a little bit each day. Similarly, as you practice kindness, you'll get a little better at it each day.

While pursuing daily kindness, be on the lookout for false teachers trying to lead you away from the truth. Always stay in the Word, and continue praying all the time so you don't fall for deceitful teachings.

And remember, if your good deeds and acts of kindness go unnoticed by the people around you, don't get discouraged. Your Father in heaven sees your good deeds and rewards them.

• •

Dear Lord, help me get better every day at being kind.
Keep me vigilant against false teachings.

A Worthy Calling

Therefore I, a prisoner for serving the Lord,
beg you to lead a life worthy of your calling,
for you have been called by God.
EPHESIANS 4:1 NLT

Imagine if the president of the United States called you personally and gave you an important mission. You would feel pretty honored and would probably be careful to get all the details of the mission right.

God has personally called you to live your life on mission. The *Westminster Catechism* describes your mission like this: "Man's chief end is to glorify God and enjoy Him forever." You glorify God by obeying His commands and praising Him in all things. You enjoy Him by recognizing what He's given you and appreciating all His blessings.

. . . .

Father God, You've put a worthy calling on my
life and given me a great mission. I want to
glorify and enjoy You in everything I do!

Flee from Sin

But as for you, O man of God, flee these things.
Pursue righteousness, godliness, faith,
love, steadfastness, gentleness.
1 TIMOTHY 6:11 ESV

Have you ever seen any of the Jurassic Park movies? In almost every movie there's a scene where a terrifying dinosaur races forward to trample someone. Instead of running away though, the person stands in place, paralyzed in fear. Everyone watching is thinking, *Don't just stand there! Run!*

When temptation and sin charge toward you, don't stand frozen in place. Run as fast as you can in the opposite direction.

Don't just run *away* from sin though. Make sure you know what you're running *toward*: rest and protection in the arms of Jesus.

. . . .

Dear Jesus, help me run away
from sin and straight to You.

The Bigger Picture

*Trust in the LORD with all your heart and lean not on
your own understanding; in all your ways submit
to him, and he will make your paths straight.*
PROVERBS 3:5–6 NIV

Have you ever been absolutely convinced you were
right about something, only to realize later that you
were actually completely wrong?

We'll never totally understand everything that's
happening in our lives or in the world. We must trust
the Lord with our circumstances, because we only see a
small part of the complete picture. God, however, sees
everything. Trust that God's directing your path, even
when you don't know where that path is going.

*Lord, I want to trust You with my whole heart.
Give me peace when Your path feels difficult.*

Out of Egypt

*"For I am the LORD who brought you up
from the land of Egypt to be your God;
thus you shall be holy, for I am holy."*

LEVITICUS 11:45 NASB

In the beginning of the Old Testament, we learn that God miraculously saved the Israelites from slavery in Egypt. Not long after escaping Egypt, the Israelites began complaining and wondering whether God still cared about them. In no time at all they'd forgotten everything God did to deliver them out of Egypt, and they began to doubt. So when God spoke to them, He reminded them that He was the same God who brought them out of the land of Egypt.

It's very easy to forget what God's already done for us when things get hard. When you feel like God isn't acting, take a moment and remember everything He's already accomplished for you.

- -

*Dear God, I'm so quick to forget all You've done
for me. When life gets challenging, remind me
of the battles You've won on my behalf.*

Misinterpreted Motives

*David said, "I am going to show loyalty to Hanun
because his father, Nahash, was always loyal to me."
So David sent messengers to express sympathy to
Hanun about his father's death. But when David's
ambassadors arrived in the land of Ammon, the
Ammonite commanders said to Hanun, "Do you
really think these men are coming here to honor
your father? No! David has sent them to spy out
the land so they can come in and conquer it!"*
1 CHRONICLES 19:2–3 NLT

Sometimes acts of kindness aren't received well. People may accuse you of having selfish motives or of using kindness to get what you want.

Continue being kind, no matter how it's taken, and pray that God changes the hearts of those around you who can't see kindness for what it is.

. . . .

*Dear Jesus, it hurts when people make fun
of me for trying to be nice. Please soften
the hearts of people who need kindness.*

My Redeemer Lives

"But as for me, I know that my Redeemer lives,
and he will stand upon the earth at last."
JOB 19:25 NLT

Do you *know* that your Redeemer lives? Do you truly believe with your whole heart that Jesus is alive?

The very same Jesus who lived, died, and rose again in the Bible still lives today. He's sitting at the right hand of God, waiting for the moment that the Father says, "It is finished!"

In that moment, Jesus will come back to earth a second time and bring everyone who trusted in Him into the new heaven and new earth.

· ·

Dear Jesus, I believe You're alive and will one day
return! Help me to always hang on to that hope.

Kindness in Human Form

*But when the goodness and loving kindness of God our
Savior appeared, he saved us, not because of works
done by us in righteousness, but according to his own
mercy, by the washing of regeneration and renewal
of the Holy Spirit, whom he poured out on us richly
through Jesus Christ our Savior.*
TITUS 3:4–6 ESV

The kindness of God took on human form when Jesus
came to earth.

No act of kindness comes close to what Jesus did
for us on the cross. Not only did Jesus sacrifice Himself,
but He gives us His Spirit—the very same Spirit that
encouraged Him and enabled Him to carry out His mission on the cross—to help us carry out our mission to
obey God and love others.

*Dear Jesus, nothing comes close to what You did
for me and all of humanity when You died on the
cross. Without Your sacrifice, we would have no
hope, and kindness would be useless. Give me
Your Spirit, and fill me with love for others.*

Cheerful Hospitality

Offer hospitality to one another
without grumbling.
1 PETER 4:9 NIV

Hospitality is the art of making someone feel comfortable in your home. It's helping your guests feel welcome, valued, and important when they're in your space.

When someone comes over to your house, take the time to show them around, offer them a drink or a snack, and introduce them to other people so they feel relaxed and at ease.

Even though you probably live with your parents or other adults right now, you can still practice creating a joyful, loving environment and cheerfully serve people who come into your home.

• •

I want people to feel welcome when they come
into my house, Lord. Give me an attitude of joy
when people come over, and help me learn how
to welcome and serve them wholeheartedly.

Don't Return to Slavery

*"We remember the fish we ate in Egypt that
cost nothing, the cucumbers, the melons,
the leeks, the onions, and the garlic."*
NUMBERS 11:5 ESV

After God led the Israelites out of slavery in Egypt, it wasn't long before their circumstances became unfamiliar and hard. Rather than rejoicing in their new freedom and trusting God, they complained about their situation and wanted to go back to Egypt because, even though they were slaves, at least they enjoyed small pleasures like fruit and fish.

Sometimes we glorify the small pleasures of sin, preferring to stay enslaved by our sinful habits rather than run toward the freedom of God's promises. Walking away from sin often feels uncomfortable and unfamiliar at first, but it's all part of the journey toward freedom in Christ Jesus.

. . . .

*Dear God, help me walk away from my sin,
even if it's uncomfortable. Give me strength
to keep walking toward freedom in Jesus.*

By His Wounds

He personally carried our sins in his body on the cross so that we can be dead to sin and live for what is right. By his wounds you are healed.
1 PETER 2:24 NLT

A few years ago, I got the flu really bad. For almost two weeks I lay in bed, too sick to even move. Now imagine if someone had come along and said, "I will take this sickness and carry it for you so you can get back to living." I'd have been incredibly foolish to say, "No thanks, I'm not that sick." Anyone who looked at me knew I was quite ill.

The sickness of sin infects everyone, but a lot of people don't acknowledge that they need healing. They think they're good enough, but really their sin is gradually killing them.

The cure for our sickness is found on the cross. Jesus took on the sickness of sin so that those who believe in Him don't have to carry it anymore.

. . . .

I know that sin has made me sick, Jesus, and the only healing is found in the wounds You suffered by dying for me. Forgive me, and heal me, Jesus!

Losing Your Life

"If you try to hang on to your life, you will lose it. But if you give up your life for my sake, you will save it."
LUKE 9:24 NLT

"He is no fool who gives what he cannot keep to gain that which he cannot lose."

Those words were said by Jim Elliot, a missionary killed while trying to reach an isolated tribe in the jungles of Ecuador during the 1950s.

Elliot and his fellow missionaries spent years learning about the Huaorani people, hoping to one day share Jesus with them. During a trip to make contact, some men from the tribe killed Elliot and his missionary team.

Elisabeth Elliot (Jim Elliot's wife) and the sister of one of the other slain missionaries continued reaching out to the Huaorani Indians. Years later, God touched the hearts of the Huaorani people and many came to know Christ. In fact, one of the men who helped kill the missionaries became a pastor.

. . . .

Dear God, I want to let go of my life and give it to You. Help me surrender temporary things and focus on the eternal treasures You've stored up for me.

Best Friends

"I no longer call you servants, because a servant does not know his master's business. Instead, I have called you friends, for everything that I learned from my Father I have made known to you."
JOHN 15:15 NIV

Do you have a best friend? Someone who knows you inside and out and will bend over backward to help you?

One sign of a good friendship is that you share things with each other. People tell things to those they care about and value.

Jesus, who calls you His friend, has shared His deepest treasure with you: the will of God the Father.

. . . .

Dear Lord, it's hard to believe that You call me "friend." Thank You for coming to earth and sharing the will of our Father in heaven.

Eye for an Eye

*"You have heard the law that says the punishment must
match the injury: 'An eye for an eye, and a tooth for a
tooth.' But I say, do not resist an evil person! If someone
slaps you on the right cheek, offer the other cheek also."*
MATTHEW 5:38–39 NLT

In movies, there's often a scene toward the end of a
film where the hero finally gets revenge on his enemy.
There's something incredibly satisfying about watching
a bad guy get what he deserves.

We love justice. In fact, our desire for justice was
placed in us by God. But "turning the other cheek"
isn't a sign of weakness. It simply shows the world that
your trust in God is greater than your need for personal vengeance.

. . . .

*Dear God, it's so hard to turn the other cheek,
but I want to put aside my desire for revenge
and trust You completely to deal with
the people who are cruel to me.*

All His Benefits

Bless the LORD, O my soul,
and forget none of His benefits.
PSALM 103:2 NASB

Several years ago, I went on a cruise for the very first time with my family. A few weeks before the trip, I went online and read about everything included in the vacation. I was so excited about all the amazing perks!

Then I noticed a little button that took me to a list of amenities and services *not* included in our vacation package—things that would cost extra money. The list was so long that, while reading it, I completely forgot what I *was* getting because I became so focused on what I *wasn't* getting.

The Lord's woven countless benefits into your life today. Don't let what you *don't* have make you forget all you *do* have in Christ Jesus.

. . . .

Lord, You're worthy of all praise, honor, and glory!
Your blessings overwhelm my life. I'm sorry
for the times I forget Your amazing gifts!

Grown-Up Faith

When I was a child, I spoke and thought
and reasoned as a child. But when I
grew up, I put away childish things.
1 CORINTHIANS 13:11 NLT

When my older sister was very young, she thought God lived in the air traffic control tower at the airport. My dad was a pilot, so our family often made trips to the airport. When my dad told us about the tall control tower, her five-year-old brain assumed it must also be where God orchestrated everything.

As she got old enough to ask questions and understand reality, my sister realized God didn't live at the airport. Now she believes the truth: God dwells in heaven but is present everywhere. Her childish belief was replaced by biblical theology.

As you get older, you'll gain a better understanding of God and His will. As you spend time with God and study His Word, your childish behaviors and beliefs will turn into a spiritually sound faith.

· ·

Dear Father God, give me wisdom and grace as I learn
to put away childish behavior and grow up spiritually.

Perseverance

Let perseverance finish its work so that you may
be mature and complete, not lacking anything.
JAMES 1:4 NIV

Many years ago, I signed up to run a marathon. In case you don't already know, a marathon is 26.2 miles of running. Or, in my case, a little running with lots of jogging and walking mixed in. I joined a running group to help keep me accountable in my training, and the coaches told us repeatedly that at some point during the race we'd be overwhelmed by the desire to quit. In those moments, they said, remember the finish line and keep moving your legs.

Perseverance means putting one foot in front of the other, knowing there's a finish line. It's focusing on doing the right thing in the moment, while remembering the ultimate goal.

There may be times in your life when you want to quit obeying God. You'll be tired, sad, and lonely, and living for Christ won't feel important. In those moments, remember there *is* a finish line, and keep going!

* * *

Dear Lord, perseverance can be so hard.
Remind me what I'm working toward, and
help me persevere in faith and kindness.

Mission Possible

"But I do not account my life of any value nor as
precious to myself, if only I may finish my course
and the ministry that I received from the Lord Jesus,
to testify to the gospel of the grace of God."
ACTS 20:24 ESV

Are you the kind of person who makes goals and then
sets out to achieve them? Or do you take things a day at
a time, trusting things will work out?

The apostle Paul had one goal that drove every area
of his life: testifying to the Gospel of Jesus Christ. That
was his mission, aim, and focus.

You can join that same mission starting right now.
Ask yourself, "How can I show Christ to the world with
my words and actions today?"

Father God, I want to live on mission for You
and for the Gospel. I'm going to do my best
to look out for opportunities to share the good
news of Jesus with those around me.

Fulfilling God's Law

Love does no wrong to others, so love
fulfills the requirements of God's law.
ROMANS 13:10 NLT

The Old Testament, also called "the Law and the Prophets," is filled with laws, prophecies, and stories about God's people. It can be confusing to know what, exactly, God wants us to take away from reading it. Fortunately, Jesus clarifies the intention of the Old Testament in the New Testament. He said, " 'Love the Lord your God with all your heart and with all your soul and with all your mind.' This is the first and greatest commandment. And the second is like it: 'Love your neighbor as yourself.' All the Law and the Prophets hang on these two commandments" (Matthew 22:37–40 NIV).

By loving others, you're fulfilling the law of God.

- -

Dear Jesus, love is such an important action.
I want to honor You by loving others.

Scouting Ahead

*"The LORD is the one who goes ahead of you;
He will be with you. He will not fail you or
forsake you. Do not fear or be dismayed."*
DEUTERONOMY 31:8 NASB

In the early years of America, settlers traveled farther west on a path called the Oregon Trail. In fact, there used to be a computer game called "The Oregon Trail" where you'd try to get your virtual wagon train to the other side of the country alive. Unlike the computer game, the actual Oregon Trail was incredibly dangerous. Obstacles, extreme weather, hostile people, and predators lurked everywhere. Groups on the Oregon Trail traveled with scouts, who ran ahead to look for dangerous conditions. Knowing about future danger allowed the wagon train to go a safer route or to carefully prepare for the treacherous terrain.

The Lord acts as our spiritual scout, going ahead of us and preparing our hearts for what lies ahead. He stays by our side in dangerous territory, guiding us and keeping us safe.

* *

*Heavenly Father, You're always going before me and
preparing me for what's next. Since You've already
navigated the path ahead, I can live in peace.*

The Real Fight

*So take everything the Master has set out for you,
well-made weapons of the best materials. And put them
to use so you will be able to stand up to everything the
Devil throws your way. This is no afternoon athletic
contest that we'll walk away from and forget about in
a couple of hours. This is for keeps, a life-or-death fight
to the finish against the Devil and all his angels.*
EPHESIANS 6:10–12 MSG

In Sunday school, we used to sing a song that went like this: "I may never march in the infantry, ride in the cavalry, or shoot the artillery. I may never fly o'er the enemy, but I'm in the Lord's army."

There's a battle happening right now, one that involves every single human being on earth: the battle for spiritual life and death. Satan wants to separate as many people as he can from God.

As a child of God, you're in His army, fighting for His righteous causes. But the weapons we use aren't made of physical materials. They're made of something even stronger: love, truth, faith, kindness, and prayer.

* *

*Father God, equip me to fight spiritual battles.
I know our battles aren't of flesh and blood, but of
spirit and truth. Make me a strong warrior for You!*

A Solid Identity

*See what kind of love the Father has given to us,
that we should be called children of God; and
so we are. The reason why the world does
not know us is that it did not know him.*

1 JOHN 3:1 ESV

Recently an old acquaintance of mine left her home to travel the world. The reason? She wanted to "find herself" so she could come back and live a full, meaningful life.

Deep down, people know that they're missing something. They try to fill that hole with adventure, relationships, achievements, or possessions. Somehow though, they always end up emptier than before.

When you firmly plant your identity in your relationship with God the Father, you'll never have to question who you are or your purpose in life. An identity built on the foundation of Christ won't ever be shaken or destroyed.

• •

*Dear God, my identity is found in You,
and You alone. I am Your beloved child,
and that gives me purpose in all that I do.*

Ministry of Reconciliation

*All this is from God, who reconciled us to
himself through Christ and gave us the ministry
of reconciliation: that God was reconciling the
world to himself in Christ, not counting people's
sins against them. And he has committed to
us the message of reconciliation.*

2 CORINTHIANS 5:18–19 NIV

When Jesus came down and took on the punishment for our sins, He reconciled us to God. To reconcile something means to settle a debt. Because Jesus paid our debt, we can stand before God free and clear, not owing Him anything. When God looks at us, He sees that we're washed clean by the blood of Jesus.

God's trusted us to get the word out about this important message. He's tasked us with telling others about the incredible exchange: Jesus' blood for spiritual freedom. What a powerful message to be entrusted with!

. . . .

*Dear God, You've given me an important message to
share with the world. People need to hear Your message
of reconciliation. Make me a minister of this good news!*

A Real Home

*"Live in me. Make your home in me just as I do
in you. In the same way that a branch can't bear
grapes by itself but only by being joined to the vine,
you can't bear fruit unless you are joined with me."*
JOHN 15:4 MSG

When I was first out of college, I rented a room from a family to save money. I soon discovered their home was an angry, stressful place. Fortunately, a family in my church invited me to live with them. They were the exact opposite of the first family. They showed kindness and hospitality, and I always looked forward to going home.

Making your home in the world is like living with the first family: stressful and unpredictable. When you put your faith in Jesus, He becomes your home. Dwelling with the Lord brings you to a place of refuge and peace.

Jesus also makes His home in you through His Holy Spirit. The more you live by obedience, love, and faith, the more comfortable your home becomes for the Holy Spirit, and He dwells with you even more.

. . . .

*Dear Jesus, make Your home in me! I want to
be a welcoming place for Your Spirit to dwell.*

A Bold Prayer

Create in me a clean heart, O God,
and renew a steadfast spirit within me.
PSALM 51:10 NASB

Right now, a new series called *Tidying Up with Marie Kondo* is trending on Netflix. In the show, a woman named Marie Kondo helps people clean out all the junk in their homes. As they get rid of unnecessary material things, they're able to live simpler, happier lives.

Perhaps one of the boldest prayers you can pray is to ask God to come in and clean out all the junk in your heart. You might be surprised by some of the things tucked away in the dark closets of your soul. As you clean out your heart, you'll feel lighter and freer to follow Jesus!

. . . .

God, I invite You to clean out the deepest parts of my heart! Help me get rid of things that weigh me down and keep me from truly knowing You.

Draw Near to God

Come close to God, and God will come close to you.
Wash your hands, you sinners; purify your hearts, for
your loyalty is divided between God and the world.
JAMES 4:8 NLT

Recently a friend told me about a golf tournament they attended in the UK. During part of the tournament, the royal family came to watch. For their safety, they were kept at a distance and no one was allowed to approach them.

It's not uncommon for royalty, politicians, and celebrities to be kept away from the general public. Fortunately, we have an open invitation to approach the Creator and Sustainer of the universe. When you go to Him, He'll come near to you. He won't stand far off when a child of His comes to Him with a need.

. . . .

Father God, I love You and I want to live a
holy life for You. Thank You for always
letting me come near to You.

The Giving Paradox

One gives freely, yet grows all the richer; another withholds what he should give, and only suffers want.
PROVERBS 11:24 ESV

I have a good friend who loves to give. She openly shares her time, home, car, and money to bless others. The strange thing is, no matter how much she gives, she never runs out. The Lord continues filling her cup, even as she pours it out for others. Furthermore, she gets incredible joy from seeing the needs of others met.

If you give everything away, it seems logical that you'd be left with nothing. The Bible, however, tells us a generous person will grow even richer. After all, you can't out-give God.

Dear Jesus, fill me up as I generously give to help others.

Proof of Faith

But someone will say, "You have faith and I have works." Show me your faith apart from your works, and I will show you my faith by my works.

JAMES 2:18 ESV

I love a good campfire. I love the crackling sound, the musky smell, and watching the smoke billow up from the flame. Here's the thing: the sound, smell, and smoke are all by-products of fire. They prove the fire is there, but they didn't start the fire.

Your works will never save you. The Holy Spirit ignites the flame of faith in your heart when you put your faith in Jesus. However, just as sounds, smells, and smoke prove there's a fire, your attitude, actions, and character prove the existence of your faith.

. . . .

Holy Spirit, I invite You to continue transforming my heart. Make my faith evident through my actions.

A Tender Heart

Finally, all of you, have unity of mind,
sympathy, brotherly love, a tender
heart, and a humble mind.
1 PETER 3:8 ESV

A couple weeks ago I heard a pastor say that getting through life takes "thick skin and a tender heart."

It's natural for your heart to break when you experience trials, challenges, and loss. As you heal, your heart will either harden or soften. Ask God to restore you in a way that makes you stronger and more compassionate. If you have a resilient spirit and a tender heart, you'll become a refuge of compassion and kindness for other people experiencing similar hurts.

• •

Dear God, give me a tender and loving
heart. When I'm hurt or cut down, heal me so
that I can trust You completely while extending
compassion and kindness to those around me.

A Stellar Reputation

*A good name is to be chosen rather than great
riches, and favor is better than silver or gold.*
PROVERBS 22:1 ESV

One of my favorite movies to watch during the holidays
is *A Christmas Carol.* (The Muppets version is my personal favorite.) The main character, Ebenezer Scrooge,
spent his life building a fortune, but he's a stingy, cranky,
and miserable man. When anyone mentions his name,
people fill with anger, fear, and pity.

People think of money and wealth as the greatest
treasure, but the best treasure is a name associated with
kindness, goodness, and love.

* *

*Dear heavenly Father, give me a name
that honors You. Make my character
a reflection of who I am in You.*

Receiving God's Blessing

"May the LORD bless you and protect you. May the LORD smile on you and be gracious to you. May the LORD show you his favor and give you his peace."
NUMBERS 6:24–26 NLT

Well, you made it to the final devotion of this book. Well done! I hope you feel encouraged and equipped to choose kindness in your daily life. You'll fall down many times on this journey, but remember you serve a God of forgiveness and grace. Don't be afraid to accept His blessings.

As you seek to live each day for Christ and pursue a life of holiness, may you experience the kindness of God, extend kindness to others, and learn to be kind to yourself in the process.

- -

Dear God, I pray that You protect me, show me favor, and grant me peace. You love me more than I'll ever know. Bless me now as I try to live a life filled with kindness.

About the Author

Kristin Weber is a writer, speaker, and comedian residing in Atlanta, GA. She wrote several years for *Sisterhood Magazine*, has co-authored two advice books for teen girls, and contributed to many popular blogs. Kristin travels all over the country giving a hilarious and powerful message about truth, culture, and identity to retreats, youth groups, camps, conferences, and more. Visit her online and be her friend at: www.kristinweberonline.com.

Inspiration and Encouragement for Your Heart

3-Minute Devotions for Teen Girls

This practical devotional packs a powerful dose of inspiration into 3 short minutes. Minute 1: scripture to meditate on; Minute 2: a just-right-sized devotional reading; Minute 3: a prayer to jump-start a conversation with God.

Paperback / 978-1-63058-856-4 / $4.99

The 30-Day Prayer Challenge for Teen Girls

This book provides a month's worth of specific, daily prayer challenges that will draw you closer to your Father God through meaningful conversation. Each day includes a devotion, scripture, questions for consideration, and prayer starters for morning, noon, and night that touch on 30 unique topics important to your heart—like friendship, school, family, school, and many more.

Paperback / 978-1-68322-709-0 / $5.99